SLAVERY AND THE BREAKDOWN
OF THE AMERICAN CONSENSUS

BASIC CONCEPTS IN HISTORY AND SOCIAL SCIENCE

Slavery and the Breakdown of the American Consensus

Edwin C. Rozwenc, Ph.D.

Chairman, Department of American Studies
Amherst College

Wayne A. Frederick

Department of History
Phillips Academy, Andover, Massachusetts

 D. C. HEATH AND COMPANY BOSTON

COPYRIGHT © 1964 BY D. C. HEATH AND COMPANY

No part of the material covered by this copyright may be reproduced in any form without written permission of the publisher. (6 L 3)

PRINTED IN THE UNITED STATES OF AMERICA

Table of Contents

SLAVERY AND THE BREAKDOWN OF THE AMERICAN CONSENSUS

A LITTLE more than a dozen years ago, the president of the American Sociological Society announced that a study of the problem of consensus was the most important way to understand social behavior. "I regard the study of consensus," Professor Louis Wirth declared, "as the central task of sociology which is to understand the behavior of men in so far as that behavior is influenced by group life."

Why should the study of consensus appear to be so important to a leading social scientist? To most of us, the word "consensus" does not seem to be so terribly important. After all, "consensus" has been a word of common use in the English language for hundreds of years. Most often we use it to indicate that there is an agreement or a common accord among the members of a committee, or among the people in a public meeting, or among the members of any political or social group that has to make decisions.

In the thinking of many social scientists, however, the concept of consensus is not exactly equivalent to the idea of agreement in the ordinary sense. They believe that the quality of agreement reached in a consensus is different from more usual forms of agreement. Consensus, they would argue, is not the same thing as a majority opinion. It is not necessarily expressed in the immediate decisions of the majority; and it has to be an agreement that includes more than a mere majority in any group or society.

This difference between mere majority decisions and consensus becomes clearer if we think of some fairly obvious examples in American politics. For instance, the election of President Kennedy by a narrow majority in 1960 should not be taken as evidence that the American consensus includes

Part 1

The
Concept
of
Consensus

all of the assumptions of the "New Frontier." Indeed, the consensus of the American people may be opposed to the large-scale spending and unbalanced budgets that would be necessary to carry out the objectives of the "New Frontier." Or to use a different type of example, there may be an overwhelming consensus of the American people in favor of expanded federal aid to education, but both houses of Congress, for various and complex reasons, seem to express a majority decision against such a measure.

Thus, consensus is a deeper and more stable kind of agreement than that which is expressed in the day-to-day decisions of the President or Congress, even in a representative democracy such as ours. The quality of the agreement that is expressed by this concept of consensus is very close to the kind of agreement that we think of when we use the word "custom." R. E. Park and E. W. Burgess in their *Introduction to the Science of Sociology* (1924) defined the concept of consensus in these explicit terms: "The continuity and life of a society depend upon its success in transmitting from one generation to the next its folkways, mores, techniques and ideals. From the standpoint of collective behavior, these cultural traits may be reduced to the one term, 'consensus'."

Nevertheless, we must not reduce the concept of consensus to a neat formula too quickly. In particular, we must not assume that consensus is something that is diametrically opposed to conflict. A consensus is not simply a social glacier made up of frozen folkways and fixed ideas; a consensus, particularly in modern democratic societies, may also be reshaped through political and social conflict.

Indeed, there are many situations in our everyday experience which illustrate this relationship between conflict and consensus. The game of football, for example, is a conflict situation of great intensity. Two teams of eleven players are engaged in a fierce and often bitter competition to see who can win the victory by scoring more touchdowns. Bones may be broken, blood may flow, and sometimes a player is killed on the field. Yet the football game operates with a highly developed consensus. There is an agreement to abide by certain rules and to accept certain penalties whether your team is winning or losing. The players on the opposing teams use the same fundamental techniques of running, kicking, passing and blocking. Moreover, the players of both teams share certain attitudes toward the game which leads them to play despite physical hazards. They may share a belief in the value of competition, of ruggedness; they may share the same desires for the elation of victory or the psychological lift of personal glory. Furthermore, the controlled conflict of a football game probably expresses

THE CONCEPT OF CONSENSUS

some of the basic values of the *American* consensus—competition, teamwork, sportsmanship, and physical vigor.

In a similar fashion, social conflicts of the right kind can be of great benefit to a dynamic society. As a matter of fact, in a democratic society, political conflict is encouraged through a competing party system that serves as a means through which the diverse groups of a complex democratic society can talk out their differences and arrive at mutual decisions and compromises.

The normal conflict of political parties and interest groups which is built into our democratic system tends to produce the day-to-day agreements and compromises which may modify and reshape the slowly developing habits and attitudes that compose a consensus. Such conflicts, indeed, have reshaped many aspects of the American consensus in our history. By means of such conflicts between management and labor, we have been able to move from patterns of violence, boycott, and blacklisting towards a consensus that favors the more orderly processes of collective bargaining. In addition we have been able to move from established habits of discrimination against immigrant groups and Negroes toward a greater degree of equality of civil rights and a greater degree of economic opportunity.

But political conflict may not always have a creative and constructive result. Whenever political conflicts reach a point at which the contending parties no longer share basic values and attitudes, then a revolution or a civil war is likely to occur. Consequently, one of the most significant problems that a historian or a social scientist can investigate in human affairs is the question of how and why a breakdown in consensus can occur in any society. And for Americans, the Civil War is the most fundamental experience in our history that can teach us something about the factors which can tear apart the political and social fabric of a great and complex democratic nation.

The study of the breakdown of consensus in any society is a complicated business, but the coming of the American Civil War is particularly puzzling. Social scientists generally assume that when a nation has a flexible social structure and a great multitude of interest groups, the diverse group conflicts tend to crisscross each other and prevent any basic cleavage from developing along one axis of controversy. The United States, in the decades before the Civil War, had apparently developed such a pluralistic and democratic social structure. The era of Jacksonian democracy had brought into American life something like universal white manhood suffrage, more devices of direct election, and participation in politics by the masses of voters. It was an age of the common man, when new groups and new social types were able to achieve social recognition and public office.

During those same years, the beginning of America's industrial revolution produced new forms of industrial organization and new regional patterns of agriculture as roads, canals, and railroads were constructed. These basic economic changes brought forth a greater variety of social groups—wheat farmers, hog-raisers, wool-growers, cotton planters, textile manufacturers, ironmasters, railroad promoters, factory workers, immigrant workers, etc.—all jostling and clamoring for various kinds of political and economic advantages. At the same time a great number of social and humanitarian reform groups appeared in response to the social tensions created by all of these changes. Thus, by the 1850's America had certainly developed a flexible social structure with a great number and variety of social groups crisscrossing each other in the political arena; and yet, as almost everyone knows, the political conflicts in America moved towards a basic cleavage along one axis.

In the decade of the 1850's, the political leaders and the political parties were no longer able to make successful compromises; they were no longer able to develop any balancing or stabilizing agreements within the American political or constitutional system. First the Whig party, one of the two major political parties between 1834 and 1854, broke apart over questions related to slavery and the Compromise of 1850. Then the Kansas-Nebraska Act of 1854 created a bitter controversy that led to the formation of the Republican party on the basis of the uncompromising principle that there should be no further expansion of slavery into the territories. In Kansas, indeed, a small-scale civil war broke out between free-soil settlers and pro-slavery settlers.

President Buchanan hoped that the Dred Scott decision by the Supreme Court in 1857 would have a stabilizing effect. But the Republican party refused to recognize the legitimacy of the decision, and Abraham Lincoln declared that the Republicans were dedicated to changing the Court's interpretation of the Constitution. When John Brown led his desperate and dangerous raid against Harper's Ferry in 1859, emotions were inflamed even more in the North and the South. As a result, the Democratic party, which had remained the only major national party with voter support in all sections, was broken into two bitterly opposed factions in 1860—the Breckinridge Democrats representing the Southern wing of the party, and the Douglas Democrats representing the Northern wing. In the final phase of the bitter political campaign of 1860, Lincoln was elected President by only a minority of the people, and his forty per cent of the popular vote was concentrated entirely in the states of the North.

The breakdown of the American consensus manifested itself in other ways as well. Some of the great religious denominations became split over the issue of slavery. The Methodists and the Baptists, two of the largest denominations, broke into separate northern and southern church organizations. Discords and withdrawals also were frequent among the Quakers and Presbyterians over questions relating to slavery. Furthermore, it became increasingly difficult to work out sectional bargains on economic issues as had been the case with tariffs, currency, and land policy during the decades before 1850. The effort to secure a homestead law was blocked by continued southern opposition in the Congress and in Buchanan's Cabinet. In addition, Northern manufacturing interests were unable to get readjustments in the tariff and banking laws. Similarly, railroad interests found their hopes for a rapid development of transcontinental railroads frustrated by the sectional deadlock in Congress. In every way, the occasions for frustration and blocked hostility multiplied, while the opportunities for safety-valve decisions of compromise and readjustment dwindled towards a vanishing point.

The main problem of this volume, then, is to discover how and why there was a breakdown in the American consensus which resulted in a civil war. Was the American consensus destroyed because of an irreconcilable moral division over the issue of slavery between the North and the South—or was the debate over slavery a disguise for other purposes? If so, what were such other purposes? Did they include a thirst for power by fanatical politicians, or the northern industrialists' drive for profit and power?

To help us answer these questions, this volume contains certain constitutional provisions and some statements by the founding fathers which provide us with the main outlines of the original consensus concerning slavery at the time of birth for the American Republic. In addition, there are several statements made by influential leaders of the major parties before the Civil War which were notable efforts to define and preserve the traditional American consensus. Another group of speeches and public declarations is included to indicate some of the ways in which the consensus was being fractured during the years of mounting crisis from 1857 to 1860. And, finally, to help us decide how we should explain the breakdown of the American consensus before the Civil War, we shall read some interpretations of the causes of the Civil War written by leading historians in the twentieth century.

When we remember that the American Civil War left a legacy of race problems, constitutional problems, and sectional conflicts that are still with us today, we can see that a study of the breakdown of the American consensus in the Civil War may lead us to a better understanding of our society. America, to be sure, is a complex and rapidly changing society and many of the problems which stem from the Civil War are being resolved or overshadowed by new issues of the twentieth century. Nevertheless, by pursuing the questions in this volume we can discover a great deal about the relationship between conflict and consensus in our democratic society that will be useful to us now and in the future.

In order to investigate the breakdown of the American consensus before the Civil War we shall need to uncover, first of all, some of the deeper roots of the mutual decisions and compromises that composed the consensus concerning slavery. In particular, we shall explore the establishment of a consensus concerning slavery at the time that the Constitution was ratified. To do this, we shall examine the provisions of the Constitution regarding slavery as well as some statements by three leading men, a Northerner and two Southerners, made during the debates over the Constitution. These documents cannot tell us all that we need to know about the consensus concerning slavery at the time of the birth of the American Republic, but they will provide us with important clues pertaining to the basic ideas of the founding fathers about the future of slavery within the constitutional system.

Part 2

The Constitutional Consensus

1. Constitutional Clauses Relating to Slavery

Historians and political scientists have often marvelled at the success of the founding fathers in framing a constitution that has endured longer than the written constitution of any other nation. One reason for the success of the founding fathers was their ability to develop workable compromises for the most serious of their differences. Some of the more troublesome issues at the Philadelphia Convention in 1787 came from sectional differences between the North and the South. Northerners thought the new government should have power to impose tariffs and regulate trade. They also thought that slaves ought to be counted in determining a state's share of direct taxes but not in determining its representation in the Congress. Southerners, on the other hand, believed that the slaves should be counted in apportioning repre-

sentation but not for direct taxation. Southerners were also afraid that Congress might interfere with slavery or the slave trade. These sectional differences were adjusted by several constitutional provisions. Read the provisions of the Constitution relating to slavery and try to answer the following questions:

1. **What was the compromise relating to representation and taxes?**
2. **What was the decision concerning the future of the slave trade?**
3. **What provision was included concerning runaway slaves?**
4. **If you consider all of these provisions together, do you think that the institution of slavery would be helped or hindered in the long run?**

ARTICLE I, Section 2, Clause 3.

Representatives and direct taxes shall be apportioned among the several States which may be included within this Union, according to their respective numbers, which shall be determined by adding to the whole number of free persons, including those bound to service for a term of years, and excluding Indians not taxed, *three fifths of all other persons.*

ARTICLE I, Section 9, Clause 1.

The migration or importation of such persons as any of the States now existing shall think proper to admit, shall not be prohibited by the Congress prior to the year one thousand eight hundred and eight, but a tax or duty may be imposed on such importation, not exceeding ten dollars for each person.

ARTICLE IV, Section 2, Clause 3.

No person held to service or labor in one State under the laws thereof, escaping into another, shall, in consequence of any law or regulation therein, be discharged from such service or labor, but shall be delivered up on claim of the party to whom such service or labor may be due.

2. A Dialogue Concerning Slavery*

On August 22, 1787, a very revealing debate took place in the Philadelphia Convention over the question of limiting the importation of slaves into the United States. The most extended remarks were made by Oliver Ellsworth of Connecticut, George Mason of Virginia and Charles Cotesworth Pinckney of South Carolina. All three were well-educated men who were very active and articulate in the Constitutional Convention. Their opinions, therefore, can give us some idea of the agreements and disagreements about slavery that existed among Americans when the Constitution was framed and ratified. Read the selection taken from James Madison's Journal of the Constitutional Convention *and consider the following questions:*

1. Which of the three men seems to be most strongly in favor of immediate measures to prevent the increase of slavery?
2. Which of the three speakers makes the strongest argument for continuing the slave trade?
3. Would you say that all three men agree that slavery is wrong and look forward to its eventual decline in America?
4. If men share similar moral ideas about slavery and disagree about the practical means of dealing with the problem, would you say that there was a reasonably clear consensus concerning slavery?

Col. Mason. This infernal trafic originated in the avarice of British Merchants. The British Govt. constantly checked the attempts of Virginia to put a stop to it. The present question concerns not the importing States alone but the whole Union. The evil of having slaves was experienced during the late war. Had slaves been treated as they might have been by the Enemy, they would have proved dangerous instruments in their hands. . . . Maryland & Virginia he said had already prohibited the importation of slaves expressly. N. Carolina had done the same in substance. All this would be in vain if S. Carolina & Georgia be at liberty to import. The Western people are already calling out for slaves for their new lands; and will fill that Country with slaves if they can be got thro' S. Carolina & Georgia. Slavery discourages arts & manufactures. The poor despise labor when performed by slaves. They prevent the immigration of Whites, who really enrich & strengthen a Country. They produce the most pernicious effect on manners. Every master of slaves is born a petty tyrant. They bring the judgment of

* From Max Farrand, ed., *The Records of the Federal Convention of 1787* (Yale University Press, 1911), II, pp. 370–372. Reprinted with the permission of the publisher.

heaven on a Country. As nations can not be rewarded or punished in the next world they must be in this. By an inevitable chain of causes & effects providence punishes national sins, by national calamities. He lamented that some of our Eastern brethren had from a lust of gain embarked in this nefarious traffic. As to the States being in possession of the Right to import, this was the case with many other rights, now to be properly given up. He held it essential in every point of view, that the Genl. Govt. should have power to prevent the increase of slavery.

Mr. Elsworth. As he had never owned a slave could not judge of the effects of slavery on character. He said however, that if it was to be considered in a moral light we ought to go farther and free those already in the Country.—As slaves also multiply so fast in Virginia & Maryland that it is cheaper to raise than import them, whilst in the sickly rice swamps foreign supplies are necessary, if we go no farther than is urged, we shall be unjust towards S. Carolina & Georgia—Let us not intermeddle. As population increases, poor laborers will be so plenty as to render slaves useless. Slavery in time will not be a speck in our Country. Provision is already made in Connecticut for abolishing it. And the abolition has already taken place in Massachusetts. As to the danger of insurrections from foreign influence, that will become a motive to kind treatment of the slaves.

Mr. Pinkney—If slavery be wrong, it is justified by the example of all the world. He cited the case of Greece, Rome & other ancient States; the sanction given by France, England, Holland & other modern States. In all ages one half of mankind have been slaves. If the S. States were let alone they will probably of themselves stop importations. He wd. himself as a Citizen of S. Carolina vote for it. An attempt to take away the right as proposed will produce serious objections to the Constitution which he wished to see adopted.

General Pinkney declared it to be his firm opinion that if himself & all his colleagues were to sign the Constitution & use their personal influence, it would be of no avail towards obtaining the assent of their Constituents. S. Carolina & Georgia cannot do without slaves. As to Virginia she will gain by stopping the importations. Her slaves will rise in value, & she has more than she wants. It would be unequal to require S. C. & Georgia to confederate on such unequal terms. He said the Royal assent before the Revolution had never been refused to S. Carolina as to Virgina. He contended that the importation of slaves would be for the interest of the whole Union. The more slaves, the more produce to employ the carrying trade; The more consumption also, and the more of this, the more of revenue for the common treasury. . . .

OUR second step in the analysis of the problem of consensus before the Civil War will be an examination of the efforts of leading Americans to preserve a national consensus against the disruptive forces that were appearing in American society a full generation after the founding fathers had guided the destinies of a newborn nation. In particular, we shall investigate the statements of Democratic and Whig leaders representing the major sections of the country—the South, the Northeast and the Northwest. As we do so, we need to bear in mind that, during the years from 1830 to 1860, the political leaders in the Presidency, in the Congress, and in the Whig and Democratic party conventions, had to discover new ways of compromising sectional differences and of readjusting the American consensus. The three selections in this part of our investigation cannot tell us all that we need to know about the complex task of readjusting a national consensus, but we will be able to discover some important and representative ideas about compromise and consensus.

Part 3

Consensus and Compromise

3. ANDREW JACKSON: Farewell Address*

Andrew Jackson, the great and popular military hero from the state of Tennessee, faced some very serious threats to national unity when he was President of the United States. In 1832, he had to deal with the crisis caused by South Carolina's nullification of the tariff laws. In the later years of his second administration, he was troubled by the violent agitation of the abolitionists in the North who were flooding the federal postal service with

* From James D. Richardson, *A Compilation of the Messages and Papers of the Presidents, 1789–1897* (Washington, D. C., 1896), III, pp. 294–298 (abridged).

newspapers and pamphlets attacking slavery, and who were pouring petitions against slavery into Congress at a fantastic rate. Consequently, when he retired from the Presidency in 1837, he thought that it was his duty to warn his countrymen against dangerous divisions and to remind them of the factors that compose a national consensus. Read the selection from Jackson's Farewell Address and try to answer the following questions:

1. **What are the dangers to the Union that Jackson emphasizes?**
2. **What does he believe is the function of the laws in maintaining unity and consensus?**
3. **According to Jackson, what remedies exist if the laws are oppressive?**
4. **What else besides the force of law does Jackson believe is necessary to maintain a harmonious consensus?**

The necessity of watching with jealous anxiety for the preservation of the Union was earnestly pressed upon his fellow-citizens by the Father of his Country in his Farewell Address. He has there told us that "while experience shall not have demonstrated its impracticability, there will always be reason to distrust the patriotism of those who in any quarter may endeavor to weaken its bands"; and he has cautioned us in the strongest terms against the formation of parties on geographical discriminations, as one of the means which might disturb our Union and to which designing men would be likely to resort.

The lessons contained in this invaluable legacy of Washington to his countrymen should be cherished in the heart of every citizen to the latest generation; and perhaps at no period of time could they be more usefully remembered than at the present moment; for when we look upon the scenes that are passing around us and dwell upon the pages of his parting address, his paternal counsels would seem to be not merely the offspring of wisdom and foresight, but the voice of prophecy, foretelling events and warning us of the evil to come. Forty years have passed since this imperishable document was given to his countrymen. The Federal Constitution was then regarded by him as an experiment—and he so speaks of it in his Address—but an experiment upon the success of which the best hopes of his country depended; and we all know that he was prepared to lay down his life, if necessary, to secure to it a full and a fair trial. The trial has been made. It has succeeded beyond the proudest hopes of those who framed it. Every quarter of this widely extended nation has felt its blessings and shared in the general prosperity produced by its adoption. But amid

CONSENSUS AND COMPROMISE

this general prosperity and splendid success the dangers of which he warned us are becoming every day more evident, and the signs of evil are sufficiently apparent to awaken the deepest anxiety in the bosom of the patriot. We behold systematic efforts publicly made to sow the seeds of discord between different parts of the United States and to place party divisions directly upon geographical distinctions; to excite the *South* against the *North* and the *North* against the *South,* and to force into the controversy the most delicate and exciting topics—topics upon which it is impossible that a large portion of the Union can ever speak without strong emotion. Appeals, too, are constantly made to sectional interests in order to influence the election of the Chief Magistrate, as if it were desired that he should favor a particular quarter of the country instead of fulfilling the duties of his station with impartial justice to all; and the possible dissolution of the Union has at length become an ordinary and familiar subject of discussion. Has the warning voice of Washington been forgotten, or have designs already been formed to sever the Union? Let it not be supposed that I impute to all of those who have taken an active part in these unwise and unprofitable discussions a want of patriotism or of public virtue. The honorable feeling of State pride and local attachments finds a place in the bosoms of the most enlightened and pure. But while such men are conscious of their own integrity and honesty of purpose, they ought never to forget that the citizens of other States are their political brethren, and that however mistaken they may be in their views, the great body of them are equally honest and upright with themselves. Mutual suspicions and reproaches may in time create mutual hostility, and artful and designing men will always be found who are ready to foment these fatal divisions and to inflame the natural jealousies of different sections of the country. The history of the world is full of such examples, and especially the history of republics. . . .

But in order to maintain the Union unimpaired it is absolutely necessary that the laws passed by the constituted authorities should be faithfully executed in every part of the country, and that every good citizen should at all times stand ready to put down, with the combined force of the nation, every attempt at unlawful resistance, under whatever pretext it may be made or whatever shape it may assume. Unconstitutional or oppressive laws may no doubt be passed by Congress, either from erroneous views or the want of due consideration; if they are within the reach of judicial authority, the remedy is easy and peaceful; and if, from the character of the law, it is an abuse of power not within the control of the judiciary, then free discussion and calm appeals to reason and to the justice of the people will not fail to redress the wrong. But until the law shall be declared void by the courts or repealed by Congress no individual or combination of individuals can be justified in forcibly resisting its execution. It is impossible that any government can continue to exist upon any other principles. It would cease to be a government and be unworthy of the name if it had not the power to enforce the execution of its own laws within its own sphere of action. . . .

But the Constitution can not be maintained nor the Union preserved, in opposition to public feeling, by the mere exertion of the coercive powers confided to the General Government. The foundations must be laid in the affections of the people, in the security it gives to life, liberty, character, and property in every quarter of the country, and in the fraternal attachment which the citizens of the several States bear to one another as members of one political family, mutually contributing to promote the happiness of each other. Hence the citizens of every State should studiously avoid everything calculated to wound the sensibility or offend the just pride of the people of other States, and they should frown upon any proceedings within their own borders likely to disturb the tranquillity of their political brethren in other portions of the Union. In a country so extensive as the United States, and with pursuits so varied, the internal regulations of the several States must frequently differ from one another in important particulars, and this difference is unavoidably increased by the varying principles upon which the American colonies were originally planted—principles which had taken deep root in their social relations before the Revolution, and therefore of necessity influencing their policy since they became free and independent States. But each State has the unquestionable right to regulate its own internal concerns according to its own pleasure, and while it does not interfere with the rights of the people of other States or the rights of the Union, every State must be the sole judge of the measures proper to secure the safety of its citizens and promote their happiness; and all efforts on the part of people of other States to cast odium upon their institutions, and all measures calculated to disturb their rights of property or to put in jeopardy their peace and internal tranquillity, are in direct opposition to the spirit in which the Union was formed, and must endanger its safety. Motives of philanthropy may be assigned for this unwarrantable interference, and weak men may persuade themselves for a moment that they are laboring in the cause of humanity and asserting the rights of the human race; but everyone, upon sober reflection, will see that nothing but mischief can come from these improper assaults upon the feelings and rights of others. Rest assured that the men found busy in this work of discord are not worthy of your confidence, and deserve your strongest reprobation.

4. DANIEL WEBSTER: The Constitution and the Union*

Daniel Webster was one of the outstanding leaders of the Whig party in the pre-Civil War period. During much of his career he was a member of the Senate from Massachusetts and well-known throughout the country for his oratorical ability. Webster was a devoted defender of the Union who often used his efforts to compromise sectional differences. At the end of the Mexican War, he was troubled greatly by the bitter controversy aroused by the attempt of the supporters of the Wilmot Proviso to exclude slavery from any of the territories acquired in the war. In 1850, moreover, many southern leaders were threatening secession, and the country faced a serious sectional crisis. Hence Webster used his prestige and influence to support the measures known as the Compromise of 1850. His famous "Seventh of March" speech was delivered in support of the principles of compromise and the preservation of the Union. Read the selection from Webster's speech carefully and consider the following questions:

1. What did Webster think was the original consensus concerning slavery when the Constitution was framed?
2. What did he think brought about a change in the consensus concerning slavery? How, in particular, had southern opinions changed?
3. What did he think was the best way to settle the question of slavery in the new territories of California and New Mexico?
4. What sentiments does Webster appeal to as binding symbols for the American people?

MR. PRESIDENT,—I wish to speak to-day, not as a Massachusetts man, nor as a Northern man, but as an American, and a member of the Senate of the United States. It is fortunate that there is a Senate

* From *The Works of Daniel Webster* (Boston, 1851), pp. 325–326, 333–334, 337–338, 350–352, 364–366 (abridged).

of the United States; a body not yet moved from its propriety, not lost to a just sense of its own dignity and its own high responsibilities, and a body to which the country looks, with confidence, for wise, moderate, patriotic, and healing counsels. It is not to be denied that we live in the midst of strong agitations, and are surrounded by very considerable dangers to our institutions and government. The imprisoned winds are let loose. The East, the North, and the stormy South combine to throw the whole sea into commotion, to toss its billows to the skies, and disclose its profoundest depths. I do not affect to regard myself, Mr. President, as holding, or as fit to hold, the helm in this combat with the political elements; but I have a duty to perform, and I mean to perform it with fidelity, not without a sense of existing dangers, but not without hope. I have a part to act, not for my own security or safety, for I am looking out for no fragment upon which to float away from the wreck, if wreck there must be, but for the good of the whole, and the preservation of all; and there is that which will keep me to my duty during this struggle, whether the sun and the stars shall appear, or shall not appear for many days. I speak to-day for the preservation of the Union. "Hear me for my cause." I speak to-day, out of a solicitous and anxious heart, for the restoration of the country of that quiet and that harmony which make the blessings of this Union so rich, and so dear to us all. These are the topics that I propose to myself to discuss; these are the motives, and the sole motives, that influence me in the wish to communicate my opinions to the Senate and the country; and if I can do any thing, however little, for the promotion of these ends, I shall have accomplished all that I expect. . . .

But we must view things as they are. Slavery does exist in the United States. It did exist in the States before the adoption of this Constitution, and at that time. Let us, therefore, consider for a moment what was the state of sentiment, North and South, in regard to slavery, at the time this Constitution was adopted. A remarkable change has taken place since; but what did the wise and great men of all parts of the country think of slavery then? In what estimation did they hold it at the time when this Constitution was adopted? It will be found, Sir, if we will carry ourselves by historical research back to that day, and ascertain men's opinions by authentic records still existing among us, that there was then no diversity of opinion between the North and the South upon the subject of slavery. It will be found that both parts of the country held it equally an evil, a moral and political evil. It will not be found that, either at the North or at the South, there was much, though there was some, invective against slavery as inhuman and cruel.

The great ground of objection to it was political; that it weakened the social fabric; that, taking the place of free labor, society became less strong and labor less productive; and therefore we find from all the eminent men of the time the clearest expression of their opinion that slavery is an evil. They ascribed its existence here, not without truth, and not without some acerbity of temper and force of language, to the injurious policy of the mother country, who, to favor the navigator, had entailed these evils upon the Colonies. I need hardly refer, Sir, particularly to the publications of the day. They are matters of history on the record. The eminent men, the most eminent men, and nearly all the conspicuous politicians of the South, held the same sentiments; that slavery was an evil, a blight, a scourge, and a curse. There are no terms of reprobation of slavery so vehement in the North at that day as in the South. The North was not so much excited against it as the South; and the reason is, I suppose, that there was much less of it at the North, and the people did not see, or think they saw, the evils so prominently as they were seen, or thought to be seen, at the South. . . .

Here we may pause. There was, if not an entire unanimity, a general concurrence of sentiment running through the whole community, and especially entertained by the eminent men of all parts of the country. But soon a change began, at the North and the South, and a difference of opinion showed itself; the North growing much more warm and strong against slavery, and the South growing much more warm and strong in its support. Sir, there is no generation of mankind whose opinions are not subject to be influenced by what appear to them to be their present emergent and exigent interests. I impute to the South no particularly selfish view in the change which has come over her. I impute to her certainly no dishonest view. All that has happened has been natural. It has followed those causes which always influence the human mind and operate upon it. What, then, have been the causes which have created so new a feeling in favor of slavery in the South, which have changed the whole nomenclature of the South on that subject, so that, from being thought and described in the terms I have mentioned and will not repeat, it has now become an institution, a cherished institution, in that quarter; no evil, no scourge, but a great religious, social, and moral blessing, as I think I have heard it latterly spoken of? I suppose this, Sir, is owing to the rapid growth and sudden extension of the COTTON plantations of the South. So far as any motive consistent with honor, justice, and general judgment could act, it was the COTTON interest that gave a new desire to promote slavery, to spread it, and to use its labor. I again say that this change was produced by causes which must always produce like effects. The whole interest of the South became connected, more or less, with the extension of slavery. . . .

Now, as to California and New Mexico, I hold slavery to be excluded from those territories by a law even superior to that which admits and sanctions it in Texas. I mean the law of nature, of physical geography, the law of the formation of the earth. That law settles for ever, with a strength beyond all terms of human enactment, that slavery cannot exist in California or New Mexico. Understand me, Sir; I mean slavery as we regard it; the slavery of the colored race as it exists in the Southern States. I shall not discuss the point, but leave it to the learned gentlemen who have undertaken to discuss it; but I suppose there is no slavery of that description in California now. I understand that *peonism,* a sort of penal servitude, exists there, or rather a sort of voluntary sale of a man and his offspring for debt, an arrangement of a peculiar nature known to the law of Mexico. But what I mean to say is, that it is as impossible that African slavery, as we see it among us, should find its way, or be introduced, into California and New Mexico, as any other natural impossibility. California and New Mexico are Asiatic in their formation and scenery. They are composed of vast ridges of mountains of great height, with broken ridges and deep valleys. The sides of these mountains are entirely barren; their tops capped by perennial snow. There may be in California, now made free by its constitution, and no doubt there are, some tracts of valuable land. But it is not so in New Mexico. Pray, what is the evidence which every gentleman must have obtained on this subject, from information sought by himself or communicated by others? I have inquired and read all I could find, in order to acquire information on this important subject. What is there in New Mexico that could, by any possibility, induce any body to go there with slaves? There are some narrow strips of tillable land on the borders of the rivers; but the rivers themselves dry up before midsummer is gone. All that the people can do in that region is to raise some little articles, some little wheat for their *tortillas,* and that by irrigation. And who expects to see a hundred black men cultivating tobacco, corn, cotton, rice, or any thing else, on lands in New Mexico, made fertile only by irrigation?

I look upon it, therefore, as a fixed fact, to use the current expression of the day, that both California and New Mexico are destined to be free, so far as they are settled at all, which I believe, in regard to New Mexico, will be but partially for a great length of time; free by the arrangement of things ordained by the Power above us. I have therefore to say, in this respect also, that this country is fixed for freedom, to as many persons as shall ever live in it, by a less repealable law

18

than that which attaches to the right of holding slaves in Texas; and I will say further, that, if a resolution or a bill were now before us, to provide a territorial government for New Mexico, I would not vote to put any prohibition into it whatever. Such a prohibition would be idle, as it respects any effect it would have upon the territory; and I would not take pains uselessly to reaffirm an ordinance of nature, nor to reënact the will of God. I would put in no Wilmot Proviso for the mere purpose of a taunt or a reproach. I would put into it no evidence of the votes of superior power, exercised for no purpose but to wound the pride, whether a just and a rational pride, or an irrational pride, of the citizens of the Southern States. I have no such object, no such purpose. They would think it a taunt, an indignity; they would think it to be an act taking away from them what they regard as a proper equality of privilege. Whether they expect to realize any benefit from it or not, they would think it at least a plain theoretic wrong; that something more or less derogatory to their character and their rights had taken place. I propose to inflict no such wound upon any body, unless something essentially important to the country, and efficient to the preservation of liberty and freedom, is to be effected. I repeat, therefore, Sir, and, as I do not propose to address the Senate often on this subject, I repeat it because I wish it to be distinctly understood, that, for the reasons stated, if a proposition were now here to establish a government for New Mexico, and it was moved to insert a provision for a prohibition of slavery, I would not vote for it. . . .

I have one other remark to make. In my observations upon slavery as it has existed in this country, and as it now exists, I have expressed no opinion of the mode of its extinguishment or melioration. I will say, however, though I have nothing to propose, because I do not deem myself so competent as other gentlemen to take any lead on this subject, that if any gentleman from the South shall propose a scheme, to be carried on by this government upon a large scale, for the transportation of free colored people to any colony or any place in the world, I should be quite disposed to incur almost any degree of expense to accomplish that object. Nay, Sir, following an example set more than twenty years ago by a great man, then a Senator from New York, I would return to Virginia, and through her to the whole South, the money received from the lands and territories ceded by her to this government, for any such purpose as to remove, in whole or in part, or in any way to diminish or deal beneficially with, the free colored population of the Southern States. I have said that I honor Virginia for her cession of this territory. There have been received into the treasury of the United States eighty millions of dollars, the proceeds of the sales of the public lands ceded by her. If the residue should be sold at the same rate, the whole aggregate will exceed two hundred millions of dollars. If Virgina and the South see fit to adopt any proposition to relieve themselves from the free people of color among them, or such as may be made free, they have my full consent that the government shall pay them any sum of money out of the proceeds of that cession which may be adequate to the purpose.

And now, Mr. President, I draw these observations to a close. I have spoken freely, and I meant to do so. I have sought to make no display. I have sought to enliven the occasion by no animated discussion, nor have I attempted any train of elaborate argument. I have wished only to speak my sentiments, fully and at length, being desirous, once and for all, to let the Senate know, and to let the country know, the opinions and sentiments which I entertain on all these subjects. These opinions are not likely to be suddenly changed. If there be any future service that I can render to the country, consistently with these senti· ments and opinions, I shall cheerfully render it. If there be not, I shall still be glad to have had an opportunity to disburden myself from the bottom of my heart, and to make known every political sentiment that therein exists.

And now, Mr. President, instead of speaking of the possibility or utility of secession, instead of dwelling in those caverns of darkness, instead of groping with those ideas so full of all that is horrid and horrible, let us come out into the light of day; let us enjoy the fresh air of Liberty and Union; let us cherish those hopes which belong to us; let us devote ourselves to those great objects that are fit for our consideration and our action; let us raise our conceptions to the magnitude and the importance of the duties that devolve upon us; let our comprehension be as broad as the country for which we act, our aspirations as high as its certain destiny; let us not be pigmies in a case that calls for men. Never did there devolve on any generation of men higher trusts than now devolve upon us, for the preservation of this Constitution and the harmony and peace of all who are destined to live under it. Let us make our generation one of the strongest and brightest links in that golden chain which is destined, I fondly believe, to grapple the people of all the States to this Constitution for ages to come. We have a great, popular, constitutional government, guarded by law and by judicature, and defended by the affections of the whole people. No monarchical throne presses these States together, no iron chain of military power encircles them; they live and stand under a government popular in its form, representative in its character, founded upon principles of equality, and so constructed, we hope, as to last for ever. In all its history it has been beneficent; it has trodden down no man's liberty; it has crushed no State. Its daily respiration is liberty and patriotism; its yet youthful veins are full of enterprise, courage, and honorable love of glory and renown. Large before, the country has now, by recent events, become vastly larger. This republic now extends, with a vast breadth, across the whole continent. The two great seas of the world wash the one and the other shore. We realize, on a mighty scale, the beautiful description of the ornamental border of the buckler of Achilles:—

> Now, the broad shield complete, the artist crowned
> With his last hand, and poured the ocean round;
> In living silver seemed the waves to roll,
> And beat the buckler's verge, and bound the whole.

5. STEPHEN A. DOUGLAS: "This Great Principle of Popular Sovereignty"*

Stephen A. Douglas belonged to the new generation of leaders which was rising to prominence in the Democratic party in the 1850's. He had played a leading role in the Compromise of 1850 and was anxious to promote the political strategies that would permit the harmonious development of railroads and the great economic resources of the West. He hoped that the Kansas-Nebraska Act of 1854 would open up the possibilities for a transcontinental railroad more rapidly, and he was appalled at the bitter sectional controversy which resulted from his cherished bill. Douglas, however, sought to restore a spirit of unity and compromise. Hence, his speeches in the famous Lincoln-Douglas debates were designed to emphasize his favorite formula for preserving a national consensus. The selection below is taken from a speech delivered by Douglas in the first debate with Lincoln in Ottawa, Illinois, August 21, 1858. Read the selection carefully and try to answer the following questions:

1. **What did Douglas think was the basis of the consensus which the Whig and Democratic parties had maintained prior to 1854?**
2. **What, according to Douglas, is the great principle which alone can maintain the American consensus in the face of the public agitation over the slavery question?**

* From John G. Nicolay and John Hay, *Abraham Lincoln, Complete Works* (New York, 1894), I, pp. 278–279, 284–286 (abridged).

Prior to 1854 this country was divided into two great political parties, known as the Whig and Democratic parties. Both were national and patriotic, advocating principles that were universal in their application. An old-line Whig could proclaim his principles in Louisiana and Massachusetts alike. Whig principles had no boundary sectional line— they were not limited by the Ohio River, nor by the Potomac, nor by the line of the free and slave States, but applied and were proclaimed wherever the Constitution ruled or the American flag waved over the American soil. So it was, and so it is with the great Democratic party, which, from the days of Jefferson until this period, has proven itself to be the historic party of this nation. While the Whig and Democratic parties differed in regard to a bank, the tariff, distribution, the specie circular, and the subtreasury, they agreed on the great slavery question which now agitates the Union. I say that the Whig party and the Democratic party agreed on the slavery question, while they differed on those matters of expediency to which I have referred. The Whig party and the Democratic party jointly adopted the compromise measures of 1850 as the basis of a proper and just solution of the slavery question in all its forms. Clay was the great leader, with Webster on his right and Cass on his left, and sustained by the patriots in the Whig and Democratic ranks who had devised and enacted the compromise measures of 1850.

In 1851 the Whig party and the Democratic party united in Illinois in adopting resolutions indorsing and approving the principles of the compromise measures of 1850, as the proper adjustment of that question. In 1852, when the Whig party assembled in convention at Baltimore for the purpose of nominating a candidate for the presidency, the first thing it did was to declare the compromise measures of 1850, in substance and in principle, a suitable adjustment of that question. [Here the speaker was interrupted by loud and long-continued applause.] My friends, silence will be more acceptable to me in the discussion of these questions than applause. I desire to address myself to your judgment, your understanding, and your consciences, and not to your passions or your enthusiasm. When the Democratic convention assembled in Baltimore in the same year, for the purpose of nominating a Democratic candidate for the presidency, it also adopted the compromise measures of 1850 as the basis of Democratic action. Thus you see that up to 1853–54, the Whig party and the Democratic party both stood on the same platform with regard to the slavery question. That platform was the right of the people of each State and each Territory to decide their local and domestic institutions for themselves, subject only to the Federal Constitution.

During the session of Congress of 1853–54, I introduced into the Senate of the United States a bill to organize the Territories of Kansas and Nebraska on that principle which had been adopted in the compromise measures of 1850, approved by the Whig party and the Democratic party in Illinois in 1851, and indorsed by the Whig party and the Democratic party in national convention in 1852. In order that there might be no misunderstanding in relation to the principle involved in the Kansas and Nebraska bill, I put forth the true intent and meaning of the act in these words: "It is the true intent and meaning of this act not to legislate slavery into any State or Territory, or to exclude it therefrom, but to leave the people thereof perfectly free to form and regulate their domestic institutions in their own way, subject only to the Federal Constitution." Thus you see that up to 1854, when the Kansas and Nebraska bill was brought into Congress for the purpose of carrying out the principles which both parties had up to that time indorsed and approved, there had been no division in this country in regard to that principle except the opposition of the Abolitionists. In the House of Representatives of the Illinois legislature, upon a resolution asserting that principle, every Whig and every Democrat in the House voted in the affirmative, and only four men voted against it, and those four were old-line Abolitionists. . . .

Mr. Lincoln, following the example and lead of all the little Abolition orators who go around and lecture in the basements of schools and churches, reads from the Declaration of Independence that all men were created equal, and then asks how can you deprive a negro of that equality which God and the Declaration of Independence award to him? He and they maintain that negro equality is guaranteed by the laws of God, and that it is asserted in the Declaration of Independence. If they think so, of course they have a right to say so, and so vote. I do not question Mr. Lincoln's conscientious belief that the negro was made his equal, and hence is his brother; but for my own part, I do not regard the negro as my equal, and positively deny that he is my brother or any kin to me whatever. Lincoln has evidently learned by heart Parson Lovejoy's catechism. He can repeat it as well as Farnsworth, and he is worthy of a medal from Father Giddings and Fred Douglass for his Abolitionism. He holds that the negro was born his equal and yours, and that he was endowed with equality by the Almighty, and that no human law can deprive him of these rights which were guaranteed to him by the Supreme Ruler of the universe. Now, I do not believe that the Almighty ever intended the negro to be the equal of the white man. If he did, he has been a long time demonstrating the fact. For thousands of years the negro has been a race upon the earth, and during all that time, in all latitudes and climates, wherever he has wandered or been taken, he has been inferior to the race which he has there met. He belongs to an inferior race, and must always occupy an inferior position. I do not hold that because the negro is our inferior therefore he ought to be a slave. By no means can such a conclusion be drawn from what I have said. On the contrary, I hold that humanity and Christianity both require that the negro shall have and enjoy every right, every privilege, and every immunity consistent with the safety of the society in which he lives. On that point, I presume, there can be no diversity of opinion. You and I are bound to extend to our inferior and dependent beings every right, every privilege, every facility and immunity consistent with the public good. The question then arises, what rights and privileges are consistent with the public good? This is a question which each State and each Territory must decide for itself—Illinois has decided it for herself. We have provided that the negro shall not be a slave, and we have also provided that he shall not be a citizen, but protect him in his civil rights, in his life, his person and his property, only depriving him of all political rights whatsoever, and refusing to put him on an equality with the white man. That policy of Illinois is satisfactory to the Democratic party and to me, and if it were to the Republicans, there would then be no question upon the subject; but the Republicans say that he ought to be made a citizen, and when he becomes a citizen he becomes your equal, with all your rights and privileges. They assert the Dred Scott decision to be monstrous because it denies that the negro is or can be a citizen under the Constitution.

Now, I hold that Illinois had a right to abolish and prohibit slavery as she did, and I hold that Kentucky has the same right to continue and protect slavery that Illinois had to abolish it. I hold that New York had as much right to abolish slavery as Virginia has to continue it, and that each and every State of this Union is a sovereign power, with the right to do as it pleases upon this question of slavery, and upon all its domestic institutions. Slavery is not the only question which comes up in this controversy. There is a far more important one to you, and that is, what shall be done with the free negro? We have settled the slavery question as far as we are concerned; we have prohibited it in Illinois forever, and in doing so, I think we have done wisely, and there is no man in the State who would be more strenuous in his opposition to the introduction of slavery than I would; but when we settled it for ourselves, we exhausted all our power over that subject. We have done our whole duty, and can do no more. We must leave each and every other State to decide for itself the same question.

In relation to the policy to be pursued toward the free negroes, we have said that they shall not vote; whilst Maine, on the other hand, has said that they shall vote. Maine is a sovereign State, and has the power to regulate the qualifications of voters within her limits. I would never consent to confer the right of voting and of citizenship upon a negro, but still I am not going to quarrel with Maine for differing from me in opinion. Let Maine take care of her own negroes, and fix the qualifications of her own voters to suit herself, without interfering with Illinois, and Illinois will not interfere with Maine. So with the State of New York. She allows the negro to vote provided he owns two hundred and fifty dollars' worth of property, but not otherwise. While I would not make any distinction whatever between a negro who held property and one who did not, yet if the sovereign State of New York chooses to make that distinction it is her business and not mine, and I will not quarrel with her for it. She can do as she pleases on this question if she minds her own business, and we will do the same thing. Now, my friends, if we will only act conscientiously and rigidly upon this great principle of popular sovereignty, which guarantees to each State and Territory the right to do as it pleases on all things, local and domestic, instead of Congress interfering, we will continue at peace one with another. Why should Illinois be at war with Missouri, or Kentucky with Ohio, or Virginia with New York, merely because their institutions differ? Our fathers intended that our institutions should differ. They knew that the North and the South, having different climates, productions, and interests, required different institutions. This doctrine of Mr. Lincoln, of uniformity among the institutions of the different States, is a new doctrine, never dreamed of by Washington, Madison, or the framers of this government. Mr. Lincoln and the Republican party set themselves up as wiser than these men who made this government, which has flourished for seventy years under the principle of popular sovereignty, recognizing the right of each State to do as it pleased. Under that principle, we have grown from a nation of three or four millions to a nation of about thirty millions of people; we have crossed the Allegheny mountains and filled up the whole Northwest, turning the prairie into a garden, and building up churches and schools, thus spreading civilization and Christianity where before there was nothing but savage barbarism. Under that principle we have become, from a feeble nation, the most powerful on the face of the earth, and if we only adhere to that principle, we can go forward increasing in territory, in power, in strength, and in glory until the Republic of America shall be the north star that shall guide the friends of freedom throughout the civilized world. And why can we not adhere to the

660007

great principle of self-government upon which our institutions were originally based? I believe that this new doctrine preached by Mr. Lincoln and his party will dissolve the Union if it succeeds. They are trying to array all the Northern States in one body against the South, to excite a sectional war between the free States and the slave States, in order that the one or the other may be driven to the wall.

IN the closing years of the decade of the 1850's, a new political crisis developed in the United States that was more severe and prolonged than any preceding crisis since the adoption of the Constitution. "Bleeding Kansas," the Dred Scott decision, John Brown's raid, the disruption of the Democratic party, and the election of Lincoln, brought sectional tensions to the breaking point and, in December of 1860, South Carolina seceded from the Union—to be followed by other southern states in succeeding months. Clearly, the American consensus was breaking down and the third step in our investigation will be to analyze some of the speeches and declarations of those years of crisis immediately preceding the secession of the southern states. The documents that we shall read are only a very small sampling of many speeches and declarations of those critical years, but they may help us to discover the ways in which political, economic and moral differences were tearing apart the bonds of consensus which had held American society together for more than half a century.

Part 4

The Breakdown of Consensus

6. ABRAHAM LINCOLN: The House Divided*

The joint debates in 1858 between Abraham Lincoln and Stephen A. Douglas in the Illinois senatorial campaign attracted widespread attention. Although Lincoln lost the election, he became a recognized leader and spokesman for the Republican party. Again and again in his debates with Douglas, Lincoln emphasized the theme that the United States was a "house divided" and that the only way to heal the division was to return to the original

* From John G. Nicolay and John Hay, *Abraham Lincoln, Complete Works* (New York, 1894), I, pp. 289–292 (abridged).

consensus of the founding fathers. The following selection is taken from Lincoln's reply to Douglas in the first joint debate in Ottawa, Illinois, August 21, 1858. Read Lincoln's statements carefully and consider these questions:

1. **Does Lincoln agree with Douglas that diversity and variety of local institutions and customs are "bonds of union"?**
2. **Why does he think that the difference over the institution of slavery must always be an "apple of discord" rather than a "bond of union"?**
3. **What, according to Lincoln, is the best way to restore sectional peace in America?**

I have no purpose to introduce political and social equality between the white and the black races. There is a physical difference between the two, which, in my judgment, will probably forever forbid their living together upon the footing of perfect equality; and inasmuch as it becomes a necessity that there must be a difference, I, as well as Judge Douglas, am in favor of the race to which I belong having the superior position. I have never said anything to the contrary, but I hold that, notwithstanding all this, there is no reason in the world why the negro is not entitled to all the natural rights enumerated in the Declaration of Independence—the right to life, liberty, and the pursuit of happiness. I hold that he is as much entitled to these as the white man. I agree with Judge Douglas he is not my equal in many respects—certainly not in color, perhaps not in moral or intellectual endowment. But in the right to eat the bread, without the leave of anybody else, which his own hand earns, he is my equal and the equal of Judge Douglas, and the equal of every living man. . . .

As I have not used up so much of my time as I had supposed, I will dwell a little longer upon one or two of these minor topics upon which the judge has spoken. He has read from my speech in Springfield in which I say that "a house divided against itself cannot stand." Does the judge say it can stand? I don't know whether he does or not. The judge does not seem to be attending to me just now, but I would like to know if it is his opinion that a house divided against itself can stand. If he does, then there is a question of veracity, not between him and me, but between the judge and an authority of a somwhat higher character.

Now, my friends, I ask your attention to this matter for the purpose of saying something seriously. I know that the judge may readily enough agree with me that the maxim which was put forth by the

28

Saviour is true, but he may allege that I misapply it; and the judge has a right to urge that in my application I do misapply it, and then I have a right to show that I do not disapply it. When he undertakes to say that because I think this nation, so far as the question of slavery is concerned, will all become one thing or all the other, I am in favor of bringing about a dead uniformity in the various States in all their institutions, he argues erroneously. The great variety of the local institutions in the States, springing from differences in the soil, differences in the face of the country, and in the climate, are bonds of union. They do not make "a house divided against itself," but they make a house united. If they produce in one section of the country what is called for by the wants of another section, and this other section can supply the wants of the first, they are not matters of discord but bonds of union, true bonds of union. But can this question of slavery be considered as among these varieties in the institutions of the country? I leave it to you to say whether, in the history of our government, this institution of slavery has not always failed to be a bond of union, and, on the contrary, been an apple of discord and an element of division in the house. I ask you to consider whether, so long as the moral constitution of men's minds shall continue to be the same, after this generation and assemblage shall sink into the grave, and another race shall arise with the same moral and intellectual development we have—whether, if that institution is standing in the same irritating position in which it now is, it will not continue an element of division?

If so, then I have a right to say that, in regard to this question, the Union is a house divided against itself; and when the judge reminds me that I have often said to him that the institution of slavery has existed for eighty years in some States, and yet it does not exist in some others, I agree to the fact, and I account for it by looking at the position in which our fathers originally placed it—restricting it from the new Territories where it had not gone, and legislating to cut off its source by the abrogation of the slave-trade, thus putting the seal of legislation against its spread. The public mind did rest in the belief that it was in the course of ultimate extinction. But lately, I think— and in this I charge nothing on the judge's motives—lately, I think, that he, and those acting with him, have placed that institution on a new basis, which looks to the perpetuity and nationalization of slavery. And while it is placed upon this new basis, I say, and I have said, that I believe we shall not have peace upon the question until the opponents of slavery arrest the further spread of it, and place it where the public mind shall rest in the belief that it is in the course of ultimate extinction; or, on the other hand, that its advocates will push it forward until it shall become alike lawful in all the States, old as well as new, North as well as South. Now I believe if we could arrest the spread, and place it where Washington and Jefferson and Madison placed it, it would be in the course of ultimate extinction, and the public mind would, as for eighty years past, believe that it was in the course of ultimate extinction. This crisis would be past, and the institution might be let alone for a hundred years—if it should live so long—in the States where it exists, yet it would be going out of existence in the way best for both the black and the white races. . . .

When I made my speech at Springfield, of which the judge complains, and from which he quotes, I really was not thinking of the things which he ascribes to me at all. I had no thought in the world that I was doing anything to bring about a war between the free and slave States. I had no thought in the world that I was doing anything to bring about a political and social equality of the black and white races. It never occurred to me that I was doing anything or favoring anything to reduce to a dead uniformity all the local institutions of the various States. But I must say, in all fairness to him, if he thinks I am doing something which leads to these bad results, it is none the better that I did not mean it. It is just as fatal to the country, if I have any influence in producing it, whether I intend it or not. But can it be true, that placing this institution upon the original basis—the basis upon which our fathers placed it—can have any tendency to set the Northern and the Southern States at war with one another, or that it can have any tendency to make the people of Vermont raise sugarcane because they raise it in Louisiana, or that it can compel the people of Illinois to cut pine logs on the Grand Prairie, where they will not grow, because they cut pine logs in Maine, where they do grow? The judge says this is a new principle started in regard to this question. Does the judge claim that he is working on the plan of the founders of the government? I think he says in some of his speeches— indeed, I have one here now—that he saw evidence of a policy to allow slavery to be south of a certain line, while north of it it should be excluded, and he saw an indisposition on the part of the country to stand upon that policy, and therefore he set about studying the subject upon original principles, and upon original principles he got up the Nebraska bill! I am fighting it upon these "original principles"—fighting it in the Jeffersonian, Washingtonian, and Madisonian fashion.

7. Reuben Davis: "Relentless avarice . . . has chained . . . the agricultural states to the northern rock."*

Reuben Davis was elected to Congress from Mississippi as a Democrat and served in the House of Representatives in the crisis years preceding the secession of the southern states from the Union. He became a leading spokesman for southern interests and frequently expressed his belief that disunion was inevitable. The following speech was made in Congress in June of 1860 just before the bitter presidential election campaign. Read the remarks of Reuben Davis carefully and try to answer these questions:

1. What does Davis think was the true basis of the original constitutional consensus?
2. According to Davis, what usurpations of power have destroyed the consensus?
3. To what extent does Davis believe that slavery is a cause of sectional discord?

At the close of the war of the Revolution, we had thirteen States. Each was a perfect government within itself. Each was a nation, with all the attributes of sovereignty, and possessed all the powers of government appertaining to a nation; had the exclusive power and right to pass laws for the regulation of its people, and to secure their rights in person and property; to declare war, make treaties, &c. Each embraced a small area of territory, similar in soil, and with the same climate. This secured the same general character of pursuits among her people, and, of necessity, created a perfect homogeneity of interest, as well as sameness of civilization, without the possibility of conflict or antagonism; and with any organism of government, giving to the people the right of suffrage, they would have been secure in having such laws adopted as were best calculated to protect them from the oppressions incident to government. And without the party discord always attendant upon antagonisms, representatives would have been elected in reference to their superior qualifications to take charge of a common interest and common welfare. Their domestic institutions would have been the same, shaped in reference to their common sentiments, and thus afforded the means of perfecting a common civilization, giving it the largest maturity and development. The necessities of the agricultural States would have been the same, and would have

* From the *Congressional Globe*, 1859–60, Part IV (Appendix), pp. 384–386 (abridged).

dictated the legislation suited to its wants. The manufacturing and mechanical States would have been in a similar condition. The same principles which guided them in shaping their laws would have given direction to their treaty engagements, so that no complaints would ever have been heard upon this continent of injustice and oppression.

Can it be supposed that those who adopted our present Federal Government intended to destroy this state of things—this homogeneity; this source of perfecting the civilization of separate communities; this guarantee against the oppressions of government; and unite under our Government the greatest variety of antagonisms, of interest, of pursuit, and of civilization, which ever existed in any Government? Manifestly not. It was not in reference to the internal wants of the States; it was not that the State had not full powers to legislate for the wants of her people; it was not to perfect the civilization of each State community, that our Federal Government was formed. Its objects were of a higher order. Its jurisdiction was intended to be extended to different and a distinct class of subjects, all appertaining to objects strictly national, and to nationalities. Its powers were intended to be limited to the common defense of all the States against foreign invasion; preserve peace between the States; raise revenue to support the Federal Government; and regulate commerce between the States and with foreign nations. The Constitution declares this to be its object and purpose; the framers of it so declared at the time; and every intelligent man must so understand it. Every well-informed man, every man conversant with the history of the formation of the Constitution, does know that the great diffculty with the convention was to discover and plan an organism for the Government which would avoid antagonism and the consequent struggle between them for the ascendancy in the Government. The members of that convention understood man sufficiently well to know that his very nature was such as to compel him to use government in such manner as would advance his own interest, although in doing so he oppressed others; that his very nature was to respect himself and his interest more than he did that of others; and that to restrain this very disposition government was found to be necessary, and from it had its origin. . . .

Now, I have said matters pertaining to individualities are with the States, while subjects national are with the Federal Government, I would have gentlemen bear this in mind. The Constitution is created by the convention; it is referred to the States; they adopt it; the first President is elected; so is Congress; the Federal Government is launched; moneyed men of this country, mere private citizens, come to Congress, and ask to have their capital incorporated to the extent of millions,† that they may use it with greater power and success in controlling the industrial pursuits of our people; that they may tax industry and labor, so as to increase their wealth and enrich themselves the more. This was asking a money monopoly, as the means of oppressing labor and all the other pursuits of man. It was the consolidation, condensation, of wealth for the oppression of others. This favor was granted. Here was a direct interference by the Federal Government with matters in their nature purely individual, and not national; and, of consequence, a departure from the terms of the compact, and a usurpation of power. Here, then, is a very early exhibition of that peculiar element in man's nature, which causes him to desire that which affects him directly, although it may prejudice others, and for the restraint of which government is founded.

Out of this question arose a party called the strict constructionists, who said this grant of power by Congress was a violation of the compact, and void; that questions like this did not belong to the jurisdiction of the Government, and were a usurpation; that Congress had no power so to consolidate the money of a half dozen men as to give them a monopoly or advantage over an unincorporated private citizen; that Congress had no power to confer upon a half dozen men the right to issue their mere paper promises to circulate as money to three times the amount of actual cash in hand; that its powers appertained to subjects national, and this was a matter of individuality. But the arguments were not heeded, and incorporated capital was made by Congress a fact, an element of power in the Government, which was thereafter to have a most controlling influence in the administration of the Government; and to appear in the politics of the country to determine and direct the suffrage of the people, and upon the floor of Congress to control its action. Of this first act of the Government, labor complained, and had the right to complain. And this very act shows how imperfect the organism of the Government was, and how almost impossible it is for human wisdom to devise a constitution of government capable of holding in check and arresting this peculiarity of man's nature to advance his own interest at the expense of others.

Next was proposed the tariff system, a measure of certainly doubtful constitutionality; and although purporting to be a revenue measure, the most unjust and unfair ever invented by a nation, it is a tax upon consumption, and therefore the most unequal and unjust ever invented. He who derives the largest amount of protection from Government should pay taxes in proportion to the protection thus received; but under this tariff system, it is often the case that the man who has

† Davis is referring here to the first Bank of the United States, chartered in 1791.

the least to protect, pays the greatest amount of tax. We frequently see persons owning thousands of dollars worth of property, which is receiving the protection of the Government, who do not consume more than the common day-laborer, who does not own one dollar's worth of property; yet, as the tax is upon what he consumes, the latter pays, for the support of the Government, more than the former. Certainly the Constitution contemplated and intended to distribute the burdens of Government equally among all the citizens of the States; and must, therefore, have looked to direct taxation. But this unfair system of taxation might have been endured without much complaint, if individual interest and cupidity had not seized upon it as a means of personal aggrandizement. Moneyed men invested in manufactures, and then demanded of the Government that the tariff should be so arranged as to give them protection against the competition of European labor. This was done; and, being done, it was but an imposition of larger taxes upon consumption, and, of course, greater burdens upon the consumer; and this not for the benefit of labor or the Government, but for men of capital; and those who made this demand upon the Government had the aid and support of that already incorporated element of power—bank capital. Thus, by the action of the Government, two formidable powers had been created, both interested in warring against the simple administration of the Government upon the limited principles of the Constitution. . . .

Well, there is created another great element of power in antagonism to the simplicity of our system of government, which is now exercising a most potent influence in the individual affairs of our people, and subjugating the suffrage to its wants. Then was introduced your system of internal improvements; harbors were to be made; rivers improved; roads built; then protection to your shipping interests, coastwise trade, &c.; until now there is not a pursuit in which man is engaged (agriculture excepted) which is not demanding legislative aid to enable it to enlarge its profits, and all at the expense of the primary pursuit of man —agriculture. And this is the only pursuit of man which cannot be benefited by legislation.

Thus it will be seen, Mr. Chairman, that the Federal Government, in direct violation of the purposes of its formation, has given legislative aid to every pursuit of man, by enabling each to impose a tax upon agriculture; and each of those interests, having a common purpose of plunder, has united and combined to use the Government as the instrument of its operation, and has thus virtually converted it into a consolidated empire. Now this combined host of interests stand arrayed against the agricultural States; and this is the reason of the conflict, which, like an earthquake, is shaking our political fabric to its foundation. To the triumph and revival of this measure of tariff, none has given more aid than the person recently warmed into existence and power by the agricultural States. Recently we have a new demandant on the stage, in the shape of the Pacific railroad, which, if built by the money of the Government, with its millions of dollars, in combination with the many hundred millions in State railroads, will be able to command, with the most despotic imperialism, the whole legislation of the country. These various interests are now acting as a unit, and, by usurpation, have sapped the very foundation of our Government; have destroyed the neutralizing elements of antagonism contained in the organization of our Government, and have virtually converted it into a consolidated empire, with general powers of legislation over every possible interest of our people.

Against this usurpation, the agricultural States still struggle, and are demanding that we shall return to the constitutional simplicity of the Union, as it was formed by the fathers of the Republic. But no; relentless avarice stands firm with its iron heel upon the Constitution, and this created incorporated power exercises despotic sway; has chained, like Prometheus, the agricultural States to the northern rock, and, as so many vultures, live upon their growing prosperity. Still these States struggle like a giant, and alarm these incorporated interests lest they may yet break the chain that binds them to usurpation; and therefore they are making this fierce onslaught upon the slave property of the southern States. From this source they expect to draw another element of power with which to overthrow, practically, the government of the Constitution—fanaticism. When they shall have done this, then we have combined the largest number of antagonisms, the largest diversity of civilization, ever embodied under any Government which has existed in the same empire. Then will be an utter destruction of all homogeneity. And then must of necessity come revolutions, wars, bloodshed, disunion, and anarchy. . . .

Mr. Chairman, I have said the various interests which I have mentioned have combined, and have substituted their mere will for the constitutional Government of our fathers, and now stand in hostile array against those who look to and defend the constitutional compact of the States. In this form we find parties now organized and arrayed. This usurpation claims the right, through Congress, to take charge of the domestic institutions of a portion of the States, and regulate them according to their peculiar and strange philosophy. They claim the right to exclude from the Territories of the United States the property of the citizens of certain States. They claim the right to destroy that property even in the States where it now exists. Those States deny both assumptions, and appeal to the Constitution to sustain them. Eighteen States, where this combination of incorporated interests exists, have united to take possession of the Government, to be wielded according to their peculiar views. The other States say they have no power to do this; that it is the Government of all the States, and must be administered for the benefit of all, and upon the principles of its organism. Out of this relation of parties grow the present impending dangers to the country; and out of it must certainly follow the dismemberment of this Republic at a very early period, unless the sober second thought of men will induce them to return to and observe the spirit and letter of our compact of government. Will you do it, gentlemen of the Republican party? You tell me, "no." Well, then, you will go on with your invasion of the agricultural industry of the country. Let me tell you, the hardy, manly, and uncorrupted tiller of the ground will not stand it. Their free spirits, elevated by the inspirations of nature, will revolt. Their proud hearts, unbent and unsubdued by the tyranny of capital, will raise a storm of resistance which no power on earth can resist. Look to it. You stand upon a mere crust, with the fires of revolution burning fiercely beneath. Look to it. Should another tread of your iron heel make but a single aperture, the flame will burst forth, and nothing short of oceans of human blood, and the desolation of this great country, can or will extinguish the flame.

8. Owen Lovejoy: "I will not curse John Brown"*

Owen Lovejoy was the brother of Elijah Lovejoy, the editor of an abolitionist newspaper who had been killed by a mob in Alton, Illinois. Elected to Congress in 1856, Lovejoy frequently expressed his abolitionist sympathies and southern representatives thought of him as a "Black Republican" of the worst sort. When he defended the motives of John Brown in a speech made in April of 1860, southern members of the House of Representatives interrupted him frequently with furious rejoinders; they could not understand how anyone could defend the mad attempt to organize an armed insurrection by Negroes in Virginia. Read the selec-

* From the *Congressional Globe*, 1859–60, Part IV (Appendix), p. 206 (abridged).

THE BREAKDOWN OF CONSENSUS

*tion from Lovejoy's speech carefully and consider the following
questions:*

1. **For what reason does Lovejoy defend John Brown?**
2. **What is Lovejoy's moral position concerning slavery?**
3. **Do you think that any consensus between the free and the slave states
was conceivable for a man like Lovejoy?**

In regard to John Brown, you want me to curse him. I will not curse
John Brown. You want me to pour out execrations upon the head of
old Ossawatomie. Though all the slaveholding Balaks in the country
fill their houses with silver and proffer it, I will not curse John Brown.
I do honestly condemn what he did, from my standpoint, and with my
convictions I disapprove of his action, that is true; but I believe that
his purpose was a good one; that so far as his own motives before God
were concerned, they were honest and truthful; and no one can deny
that he stands head and shoulders above any other character that appeared on the stage in that tragedy from beginning to end; from the
time he entered the armory there to the time when he was strangled by
Governor "Fussation." [General laughter.]

He was not guilty of murder or treason. He did unquestionably violate the statute against aiding slaves to escape; but no blood was shed,
except by the panic-stricken multitude, till Stevens was fired upon
while waving a flag of truce. The only murder was that of Thompson,
who was snatched from the heroic protection of a woman, and riddled
with balls at the railroad bridge. Despotism has seldom sacrificed
three nobler victims than Brown, Stevens, and Hazlitt.

As I remarked, Mr. Chairman, this brings us to confront slavery, and
ask what right this Caliban has upon earth? I say no right. My honest
conviction—and I do not know why gentlemen need take offense; they
need not unless they choose—my honest conviction is, that all these
slaveholding laws have the same moral power and force that rules
among pirates have for the distribution of their booty; that regulations
among robbers have for the division of their spoils; and although I do
not believe gentlemen have behaved very handsomely to me, I am
going to add, notwithstanding, that I do not mean to say that gentlemen who are slaveholders would be guilty of these particular things—
that is not the point—I am talking about this matter in the court of
conscience, in the court of right and wrong; and I insist that any laws
for enslaving men have just the same moral force as the arrangement
among robbers and pirates for distributing their spoils.

I want to know by what right you can come and make me a slave?
I want to know by what right you can say that my child shall be your
slave? I want to know by what right you say that the mother shall not
have her child, given to her from God through the martyrdom of mater-
nity? Hear that soft exquisite warble of a mother's love:

> Ere last year's sun had left the sky,
> A birdling sought my Indian nest,
> And folded, ah! so lovingly,
> Its tiny wings upon my breast.†

Now where is the wretch who would dare to go up and take that
fluttering and panting birdling from the bosom of its mother, and say,
"It is mine; I will sell it like a calf; I will sell it like a pig?" What right
had that mother to her babe? Was it because she was "Fanny Forrester," the gifted authoress; was it because she was the wife of a vener-
able and venerated missionary? No, it was because she was its MOTHER;
and every slave mother has just as good a title to *her* babe as "Fanny
Forrester" had to hers. No laws can make it right to rob her. I say, in
God's name, my child is mine; and yet I have no right to mine that a
slave father has not to his child. Not a particle. The same argument
that proves my right to my personal liberty, proves the right of every
human being to his. The argument that proves my right to my children,
gives the same title, the same sacred claim to every father. They, as I,
get it from their God, and no human enactment can annul the claim.
No, sir, never! Therefore, every slave has a right to his freedom, in
spite of your slave laws. Every slave has a right to run away, in spite
of your slave laws.

I tell you, Mr. Chairman, and I tell you all, that if I were a slave,
and had I the power, and were it necessary to achieve my freedom, I
would not hesitate to fill up and bridge over the chasm that yawns between the hell of slavery and the heaven of freedom with the carcasses
of the slain. Give me my freedom. Hands off. Unthrottle that man.
Give him his liberty. He is entitled to it from his God. With these
views, I do not think, of course, it is any harm to help away a slave.
I told you that a year ago. I need not repeat it. . . .

---

† Lovejoy is quoting lines from a poem written under the pen name of "Fanny Forrester" by
Emily Chubbuck Judson, wife of a noted Christian missionary who had served in Burma.

9. The Republican Platform of 1860

In May of 1860, the Republican party held its national convention in Chicago, Illinois, and nominated Abraham Lincoln as its candidate for President of the United States. The platform which was adopted by the Republican party in 1860 was a particularly important document because it indicated how the Republicans intended to use their power if they should win control of the national government. Read the provisions of the Republican platform with great care and try to answer the following questions:

1. What does the platform say about the rights of the states to control their own "domestic institutions"?
2. What position does the Republican party take regarding the expansion of slavery into the territories?
3. What does the platform have to say about the constitutional doctrine, established in the Dred Scott decision, that slave property should be protected in any or all of the territories of the United States?
4. Would you say that the provisions relating to slavery in the Republican platform made any hope for a national consensus impossible?
5. What provisions of an economic nature were included in the Republican platform?
6. Would you say that the economic provisions of the Republican platform are more important than the provisions concerning slavery? Why, or why not?

REPUBLICAN PLATFORM.

Resolved, That we, the delegated representatives of the Republican electors of the United States, in convention assembled, in discharge of the duty we owe to our constituents and our country, unite in the following declarations:

1. That the history of the nation during the last four years has fully established the propriety and necessity of the organization and perpetuation of the Republican party, and that the causes which called it into existence are permanent in their nature, and now, more than ever before, demand its peaceful and constitutional triumph.

2. That the maintenance of the principles promulgated in the Declaration of Independence and embodied in the federal Constitution, "That all men are created equal; that they are endowed by their Creator with certain inalienable rights; that among these are life, liberty, and the pursuit of happiness; that to secure these rights, governments are instituted among men, deriving their just powers from the consent of the governed,"—is essential to the preservation of our republican institutions; and that the federal Constitution, the rights of the states, and the union of the states must and shall be preserved.

3. That to the union of the states this nation owes its unprecedented increase in population, its surprising development of material resources, its rapid augmentation of wealth, its happiness at home and its honor abroad; and we hold in abhorrence all schemes for disunion, come from whatever source they may; and we congratulate the country that no Republican member of Congress has uttered or countenanced the threats of disunion so often made by Democratic members, without rebuke and with applause from their political associates; and we denounce those threats of disunion, in case of a popular overthrow of their ascendency, as denying the vital principles of a free government, and as an avowal of contemplated treason, which it is the imperative duty of an indignant people sternly to rebuke and forever silence.

4. That the maintenance inviolate of the rights of the states, and especially the right of each state to order and control its own domestic institutions according to its own judgment exclusively, is essential to that balance of power on which the perfection and endurance of our political fabric depends; and we denounce the lawless invasion by armed force of the soil of any state or territory, no matter under what pretext, as among the gravest of crimes.

5. That the present Democratic administration has far exceeded our worst apprehensions, in its measureless subserviency to the exactions of a sectional interest, as especially evinced in its desperate exertions to force the infamous Lecompton constitution upon the protesting people of Kansas; in construing the personal relations between master and servant to involve an unqualified property in persons; in its attempted enforcement everywhere, on land and sea, through the intervention of Congress and of the federal courts, of the extreme pretensions of a purely local interest; and in its general and unvarying abuse of the power intrusted to it by a confiding people.

6. That the people justly view with alarm the reckless extravagance which pervades every department of the federal government; that a return to rigid economy and accountability is indispensable to arrest the systematic plunder of the public treasury by favored partisans, while the recent startling developments of frauds and corruptions at the federal metropolis show that an entire change of administration is imperatively demanded.

7. That the new dogma,—that the Constitution, of its own force, carries slavery into any or all of the territories of the United States,— is a dangerous political heresy, at variance with the explicit provisions of that instrument itself, with contemporaneous exposition, and with legislative and judicial precedent; is revolutionary in its tendency and subversive of the peace and harmony of the country.

8. That the normal condition of all the territory of the United States is that of freedom; that, as our republican fathers, when they had abolished slavery in all our national territory, ordained that "no person should be deprived of life, liberty, or property without due process of law," it becomes our duty, by legislation, whenever such legislation is necessary, to maintain this provision of the Constitution against all attempts to violate it; and we deny the authority of Congress, of a territorial legislature, or of any individuals, to give legal existence to slavery in any territory of the United States.

9. That we brand the recent reopening of the African slave trade, under the cover of our national flag, aided by perversions of judicial power, as a crime against humanity and a burning shame to our country and age; and we call upon Congress to take prompt and efficient measures for the total and final suppression of that execrable traffic.

10. That in the recent vetoes, by their federal governors, of the acts of the legislatures of Kansas and Nebraska, prohibiting slavery in those territories, we find a practical illustration of the boasted Democratic principle of non-intervention and popular sovereignty, embodied in the Kansas-Nebraska Bill, and a demonstration of the deception and fraud involved therein.

11. That Kansas should of right be immediately admitted as a state under the constitution recently formed and adopted by her people and accepted by the House of Representatives.

12. That, while providing revenue for the support of the general government by duties upon imports, sound policy requires such an adjustment of these imposts as to encourage the development of the industrial interests of the whole country; and we commend that policy of national exchanges which secures to the workingmen liberal wages, to agriculture remunerative prices, to mechanics and manufacturers an adequate reward for their skill, labor, and enterprise, and to the nation commercial prosperity and independence.

13. That we protest again any sale or alienation to others of the public lands held by actual settlers, and against any view of the free-homestead policy which regards the settlers as paupers or suppliants for public bounty; and we demand the passage by Congress of the complete and satisfactory homestead measure which has already passed the House.

14. That the Republican party is opposed to any change in our naturalization laws, or any state legislation by which the rights of citizens hitherto accorded to immigrants from foreign lands shall be abridged or impaired; and in favor of giving a full and efficient pro-

tection to the rights of all classes of citizens, whether native or naturalized, both at home and abroad.

15. That appropriations by Congress for river and harbor improvements of a national character, required for the accommodation and security of an existing commerce, are authorized by the Constitution and justified by the obligation of government to protect the lives and property of its citizens.

16. That a railroad to the Pacific Ocean is imperatively demanded by the interests of the whole country; that the federal government ought to render immediate and efficient aid in its construction; and that, as preliminary thereto, a daily overland mail should be promptly established.

17. Finally, having thus set forth our distinctive principles and views, we invite the co-operation of all citizens, however differing on other questions, who substantially agree with us in their affirmance and support.

10. Declaration of the Causes which Induced the Secession of South Carolina*

After the election of Lincoln to the Presidency in November of 1860, South Carolina took the lead in fulfilling the frequent warnings that the southern states would withdraw from the Union if the Republican party won control of the federal government. On December 20, 1860, a convention in that state formally adopted an ordinance of secession. At the same time, a Declaration was drawn up to explain to the world the causes which had induced South Carolina to take this step. Read the South Carolina Declaration with great care and consider the following questions:

1. How does the South Carolina Declaration define the rights of the states under the Constitution?
2. What is emphasized in the Declaration as the main cause that has broken the "constitutional compact"?

* From Frank Moore (ed.), *The Rebellion Record* (New York, 1861), Vol. I, pp. 3–4.

The people of the State of South Carolina in Convention assembled, on the 2d day of April, A. D. 1852, declared that the frequent violations of the Constitution of the United States by the Federal Government, and its encroachments upon the reserved rights of the States, fully justified this State in their withdrawal from the Federal Union; but in deference to the opinions and wishes of the other Slaveholding States, she forbore at that time to exercise this right. Since that time these encroachments have continued to increase, and further forbearance ceases to be a virtue.

And now the State of South Carolina having resumed her separate and equal place among nations, deems it due to herself, to the remaining United States of America, and to the nations of the world, that she should declare the immediate causes which have led to this act.

In the year 1765, that portion of the British Empire embracing Great Britain undertook to make laws for the Government of that portion composed of the thirteen American Colonies. A struggle for the right of self-government ensued, which resulted, on the 4th of July 1776, in a Declaration, by the Colonies, "that they are, and of right ought to be, FREE AND INDEPENDENT STATES; and that, as free and independent States, they have full power to levy war, conclude peace, contract alliances, establish commerce, and to do all other acts and things which independent States may of right do."

They further solemnly declared that whenever any "form of government becomes destructive of the ends for which it was established, it is the right of the people to alter or abolish it, and to institute a new government." Deeming the Government of Great Britain to have become destructive of these ends, they declared that the Colonies "are absolved from all allegiance to the British Crown, and that all political connection between them and the State of Great Britain is, and ought to be, totally dissolved."

In pursuance of this Declaration of Independence, each of the thirteen States proceeded to exercise its separate sovereignty; adopted for itself a Constitution, and appointed officers for the administration of government in all its departments—Legislative, Executive and Judicial. For purposes of defense they united their arms and their counsel; and, in 1778, they entered into a League known as the Articles of Confederation, whereby they agreed to entrust the administration of their external relations to a common agent, known as the Congress of the United States, expressly declaring, in the first article, "that each State retains its sovereignty, freedom and independence, and every power, jurisdiction and right which is not, by this Confederation, expressly delegated to the United States in Congress assembled."

Under this Confederation the War of the Revolution was carried on; and on the 3d of September, 1783, the contest ended, and a definite Treaty was signed by Great Britain, in which she acknowledged the Independence of the Colonies in the following terms:

ARTICLE 1. His Britannic Majesty acknowledges the said United States, viz.: New Hampshire, Massachusetts Bay, Rhode Island and Providence Plantations, Connecticut, New York, New Jersey, Pennsylvania, Delaware, Maryland, Virginia, North Carolina, South Carolina and Georgia, to be FREE, SOVEREIGN, AND INDEPENDENT STATES; that he treats with them as such; and, for himself, his heirs and successors, relinquishes all claims to the government, propriety, and territorial rights of the same and every part thereof.

Thus were established the two great principles asserted by the Colonies, namely, the right of a State to govern itself, and the right of a people to abolish a Government when it becomes destructive of the ends for which it was instituted. And concurrent with the establishment of these principles, was the fact, that each Colony became and was recognized by the mother country as a FREE, SOVEREIGN, AND INDEPENDENT STATE.

In 1787, Deputies were appointed by the States to revise the articles of Confederation; and on 17th September, 1787, these Deputies recommended, for the adoption of the States, the Articles of Union, known as the Constitution of the United States.

The parties to whom this constitution was submitted were the several sovereign States; they were to agree or disagree, and when nine of them agreed, the compact was to take effect among those concurring; and the General Government, as the common agent, was then to be invested with their authority.

If only nine of the thirteen States had concurred, the other four would have remained as they then were—separate, sovereign States, independent of any of the provisions of the Constitution. In fact, two of the States did not accede to the Constitution until long after it had gone into operation among the other eleven; and during that interval, they each exercised the functions of an independent nation.

By this Constitution, certain duties were imposed upon the several States, and the exercise of certain of their powers was restrained, which necessarily impelled their continued existence as sovereign states. But, to remove all doubt, an amendment was added, which declared that the powers not delegated to the United States by the Constitution, nor prohibited by it to the States, are reserved to the States respectively, or to the people. On the 23d May, 1788, South Carolina, by a Convention of her people, passed an ordinance assenting to this Constitution, and afterwards altered her own Constitution to conform herself to the obligations she had undertaken.

Thus was established, by compact between the States, a Government with defined objects and powers, limited to the express words of the grant. This limitation left the whole remaining mass of power subject to the clause reserving it to the States or the people, and rendered unnecessary any specification of reserved rights. We hold that the Government thus established is subject to the two great principles asserted in the Declaration of Independence; and we hold further, that the mode of its formation subjects it to a third fundamental principle, namely, the law of compact. We maintain that in every compact between two or more parties, the obligation is mutual; that the failure of one of the contracting parties to perform a material part of the agreement, entirely releases the obligation of the other; and that, where no arbiter is provided, each party is remitted to his own judgment to determine the fact of failure, with all its consequences.

In the present case, that fact is established with certainty. We assert that fourteen of the States have deliberately refused for years past to fulfill their constitutional obligations, and we refer to their own statutes for the proof.

The Constitution of the United States, in its fourth Article, provides as follows:

> No person held to service or labor in one State under the laws thereof, escaping into another, shall, in consequence of any law or regulation therein, be discharged from such service or labor, but shall be delivered up, on claim of the party to whom such service or labor may be due.

This stipulation was so material to the compact that without it that compact would not have been made. The greater number of the contracting parties held slaves, and they had previously evinced their estimate of the value of such a stipulation by making it a condition in the Ordinance for the government of the territory ceded by Virginia, which obligations, and the laws of the General Government, have ceased to effect the objects of the Constitution. The States of Maine, New Hampshire, Vermont, Massachusetts, Connecticut, Rhode Island, New York, Pennsylvania, Illinois, Indiana, Michigan, Wisconsin, and Iowa, have enacted laws which either nullify the acts of Congress, or render useless any attempt to execute them. In many of these States the fugitive is discharged from the service of labor claimed, and in none of them has the State Government complied with the stipulation made in the Constitution. The State of New Jersey, at an early day, passed a law in conformity with her constitutional obligation; but the current of Anti-Slavery feeling has led her more recently to enact laws which render inoperative the remedies provided by her own laws and by the laws of Congress. In the State of New York even the right of transit for a slave has been denied by her tribunals; and the States of Ohio and Iowa have refused to surrender to justice fugitives charged with murder, and with inciting servile insurrection in the State of Virginia. Thus the constitutional compact has been deliberately broken and disregarded by the non-slaveholding States; and the consequence follows that South Carolina is released from her obligation.

The ends for which this Constitution was framed are declared by itself to be "to form a more perfect union, to establish justice, insure domestic tranquillity, provide for the common defense, promote the general welfare, and secure the blessings of liberty to ourselves and our posterity."

These ends it endeavored to accomplish by a Federal Government, in which each State was recognized as an equal, and had separate control over its own institutions. The right of property in slaves was recognized by giving to free persons distinct political rights; by giving them the right to represent, and burdening them with direct taxes for, three-fifths of their slaves; by authorizing the importation of slaves for twenty years; and by stipulating for the rendition of fugitives from labor.

We affirm that these ends for which this Government was instituted have been defeated, and the Government itself has been destructive of them by the action of the non-slaveholding States. Those States have assumed the right of deciding upon the propriety of our domestic institutions; and have denied the rights of property established in fifteen of the States and recognized by the Constitution; they have denounced as sinful the institution of Slavery; they have permitted the open establishment among them of societies, whose avowed object is to disturb the peace of and eloin the property of the citizens of other States. They have encouraged and assisted thousands of our slaves to leave their homes; and those who remain, have been incited by emissaries, books, and pictures, to servile insurrection.

For twenty-five years this agitation has been steadily increasing, until it has now secured to its aid the power of the common Government. Observing the *forms* of the Constitution, a sectional party has found within that article establishing the Executive Department, the means of subverting the Constitution itself. A geographical line has been drawn across the Union, and all the States north of that line have united in the election of a man to the high office of President of the

THE BREAKDOWN OF CONSENSUS

United States whose opinions and purposes are hostile to Slavery. He is to be entrusted with the administration of the common Government, because he has declared that that "Government cannot endure permanently half slave, half free," and that the public mind must rest in the belief that Slavery is in the course of ultimate extinction.

This sectional combination for the subversion of the Constitution has been aided, in some of the States, by elevating to citizenship persons who, by the supreme law of the land, are incapable of becoming citizens; and their votes have been used to inaugurate a new policy, hostile to the South, and destructive of its peace and safety.

On the 4th of March next this party will take possession of the Government. It has announced that the South shall be excluded from the common territory, that the Judicial tribunal shall be made sectional, and that a war must be waged against Slavery until it shall cease throughout the United States.

The guarantees of the Constitution will then no longer exist; the equal rights of the States will be lost. The Slaveholding States will no longer have the power of self-government, or self-protection, and the Federal Government will have become their enemy.

Sectional interest and animosity will deepen the irritation; and all hope of remedy is rendered vain, by the fact that the public opinion at the North has invested a great political error with the sanctions of a more erroneous religious belief.

We, therefore, the people of South Carolina, by our delegates in Convention assembled, appealing to the Supreme Judge of the world for the rectitude of our intentions, have solemnly declared that the Union heretofore existing between this State and the other States of North America is dissolved, and that the State of South Carolina has resumed her position among the nations of the world, as a separate and independent state, with full power to levy war, conclude peace, contract alliances, establish commerce, and to do all other acts and things which independent States may of right do.

In our final group of readings, we shall be examining the explanations for the breakdown of the American consensus that have been made by some twentieth-century historians. All three of the writers in this section have read some of the same documents that are included in this volume and many others besides. Sometimes they may even refer to some of the documents that you have just read.

The interpretations by these historians are developed with the assumption that the reader already knows something about the events of the pre-Civil War period. Thus, as you read their explanations, it would be well for you to remember what you already know about the historical events of the pre-Civil War period as well as what you have learned about the problems of consensus from your reading of the previous selections in this volume. The following chronological list of events is included to help you refresh your historical memory.

1850   Congress passes a series of acts known as the Compromise of 1850.

1851   Calhoun proposes his theory of "concurrent majorities." Donald McKay's *Flying Cloud* was launched, inaugurating the Era of the Clipper Ship trade.
The river steamboat trade reaches its peak.

1852   Franklin Pierce, a Democrat, is elected President.
Harriet Beecher Stowe writes *Uncle Tom's Cabin*.

1854   Congress passes the Kansas-Nebraska Act and repeals the Missouri Compromise agreed to in 1820.
The Ostend Manifesto is declared. Commodore Matthew Perry opens Japan to American trade.

Part 5

The Breakdown of Consensus as Explained by Twentieth-Century Historians

The first east-west railroad reaches the Mississippi River.

George Fitzhugh writes *Sociology for the South* (an apology for slavery).

The Republican party is founded.

1855   A railroad across the isthmus of Panama is completed.

The Saulte-Ste. Marie Canal is completed, linking all the Great Lakes for east-west commerce.

1856   The Republican party enters its first Presidential election.

The violence of "bleeding Kansas" reaches its height in the sacking of Lawrence and John Brown's retaliations.

Charles Sumner delivers his speech on the "Crime Against Kansas," and is later assaulted in the Senate chamber by Representative Brooks.

James Buchanan, a Democrat, is elected President.

Chicago becomes the leading railroad center of the nation.

1857   Hinton Helper, a North Carolinian, writes *The Impending Crisis of the South* (an analysis of the evils of slavery).

Roger B. Taney hands down his opinion in the *Dred Scott v. Sanford* case.

A severe economic panic begins.

1858   The Lincoln-Douglas debates are held.

1859   James Hammond of South Carolina declares "Cotton is King."

John Brown raids the U. S. Arsenal at Harper's Ferry, Virginia.

1860   Five east-west railroads have now reached the Mississippi River.

The Democratic party divides into two parties.

Abraham Lincoln, a Republican, is elected President.

South Carolina secedes from the Union.

11. CHARLES A. BEARD: The Approach of the Irrepressible Conflict*

Charles A. Beard's The Rise of American Civilization *was published in 1927 and, for more than a decade, Beard's historical interpretation had a very great influence on the teaching and*

* Reprinted with the permission of the publisher from Vol. II, pp. 3–13, 36–40, 51, of *The Rise of American Civilization* by Charles A. Beard. Copyright 1927, 1930 and 1933 by The Macmillan Company. Renewed 1955, 1958 by Mary Beard, 1963 by William Beard and Miriam B. Uagts.

writing of American history. His chapters on the Civil War era were among those which stirred considerable debate among scholars. Beard was primarily interested in economic institutions and economic influences in his method of historical interpretation, and this is clearly evident in his chapter on the approach of the Civil War. Read the following selection from that chapter with these questions in mind:

1. **What evidence does Beard find for a conflict of "vital economic interests"?**
2. **What arguments does he use to demonstrate that "it seems reasonable to assume that the institution of slavery was not the fundamental issue during the epoch preceding the bombardment of Fort Sumter"?**

Had the economic systems of the North and the South remained static or changed slowly without effecting immense dislocations in the social structure, the balance of power might have been maintained indefinitely by repeating the compensatory tactics of 1787, 1820, 1833, and 1850; keeping in this manner the inherent antagonisms within the bounds of diplomacy. But nothing was stable in the economy of the United States or in the moral sentiments associated with its diversities.

Within each section of the country, the necessities of the productive system were generating portentous results. The periphery of the industrial vortex of the Northeast was daily enlarging, agriculture in the Northwest was being steadily supplemented by manufacturing, and the area of virgin soil open to exploitation by planters was diminishing with rhythmic regularity—shifting with mechanical precision the weights which statesmen had to adjust in their efforts to maintain the equilibrium of peace. Within each of the three sections also occurred an increasing intensity of social concentration as railways, the telegraph, and the press made travel and communication cheap and almost instantaneous, facilitating the centripetal process that was drawing people of similar economic status and parallel opinions into cooperative activities. Finally the intellectual energies released by accumulating wealth and growing leisure—stimulated by the expansion of the reading public and the literary market—developed with deepened accuracy the word-patterns of the current social persuasions, contributing with galvanic effect to the consolidation of identical groupings.

As the years passed, the planting leaders of Jefferson's agricultural party insisted with mounting fervor that the opposition, first of the

50   THE BREAKDOWN OF CONSENSUS

Whigs and then of the Republicans, was at bottom an association of interests formed for the purpose of plundering productive management and labor on the land. And with steadfast insistence they declared that in the insatiable greed of their political foes lay the source of the dissensions which were tearing the country asunder.

"There is not a pursuit in which man is engaged (agriculture excepted)," exclaimed Reuben Davis of Mississippi in 1860, "which is not demanding legislative aid to enable it to enlarge its profits and all at the expense of the primary pursuit of man—agriculture. . . . Those interests, having a common purpose of plunder, have united and combined to use the government as the instrument of their operation and have thus virtually converted it into a consolidated empire. Now this combined host of interests stands arrayed against the agricultural states; and this is the reason of the conflict which like an earthquake is shaking our political fabric to its foundation." The furor over slavery is a mere subterfuge to cover other purposes. "Relentless avarice stands firm with its iron heel upon the Constitution." This creature, "incorporated avarice," has chained "the agricultural states to the northern rock" and lives like a vulture upon their prosperity. It is the effort of Prometheus to burst his manacles that provokes the assault on slavery. "These states struggle like a giant," continued Davis, "and alarm these incorporated interests, lest they may break the chain that binds them to usurpation; and therefore they are making this fierce onslaught upon the slave property of the southern states."

The fact that free-soil advocates waged war only on slavery in the territories was to Jefferson Davis conclusive proof of an underlying conspiracy against agriculture. He professed more respect for the abolitionist than for the free-soiler. The former, he said, is dominated by an honest conviction that slavery is wrong everywhere and that all men ought to be free; the latter does not assail slavery in the states— he merely wishes to abolish it in the territories that are in due course to be admitted to the Union.

With challenging directness, Davis turned upon his opponents in the Senate and charged them with using slavery as a blind to delude the unwary: "What do you propose, gentlemen of the Free-Soil party? Do you propose to better the condition of the slave? Not at all. What then do you propose? You say you are opposed to the expansion of slavery. . . . Is the slave to be benefited by it? Not at all. It is not humanity that influences you in the position which you now occupy before the country. . . . It is that you may have an opportunity of cheating us that you want to limit slave territory within circumscribed bounds. It is that you may have a majority in the Congress of the

United States and convert the Government into an engine of northern aggrandizement. It is that your section may grow in power and prosperity upon treasures unjustly taken from the South, like the vampire bloated and gorged with the blood which it has secretly sucked from its victim . . . You desire to weaken the political power of the southern states; and why? Because you want, by an unjust system of legislation, to promote the industry of the New England states, at the expense of the people of the South and their industry."

Such in the mind of Jefferson Davis, fated to be president of the Confederacy, was the real purpose of the party which sought to prohibit slavery in the territories; that party did not declare slavery to be a moral disease calling for the severe remedy of the surgeon; it merely sought to keep bondage out of the new states as they came into the Union—with one fundamental aim in view, namely, to gain political ascendancy in the government of the United States and fasten upon the country an economic policy that meant the exploitation of the South for the benefit of northern capitalism.

But the planters were after all fighting against the census returns, as the phrase of the day ran current. The amazing growth of northern industries, the rapid extension of railways, the swift expansion of foreign trade to the ends of the earth, the attachment of the farming regions of the West to the centers of manufacture and finance through transportation and credit, the destruction of state consciousness by migration, the alien invasion, the erection of new commonwealths in the Valley of Democracy, the nationalistic drive of interstate commerce, the increase of population in the North, and the southward pressure of the capitalistic glacier all conspired to assure the ultimate triumph of what the orators were fond of calling "the free labor system." This was a dynamic thrust far too powerful for planters operating in a limited territory with incompetent labor on soil of diminishing fertility. Those who swept forward with it, exulting in the approaching triumph of machine industry, warned the planters of their ultimate subjection.

To statesmen of the invincible forces recorded in the census returns, the planting opposition was a huge, compact, and self-conscious economic association bent upon political objects—the possession of the government of the United States, the protection of its interests against adverse legislation, dominion over the territories, and enforcement of the national fugitive slave law throughout the length and breadth of the land. No phrase was more often on the lips of northern statesmen than "the slave power." The pages of the Congressional Globe bristled with references to "the slave system" and its influence over the government of the country. But it was left for William H. Seward of New York to describe it with a fullness of familiar knowledge that made his characterization a classic.

Seward knew from experience that a political party was no mere platonic society engaged in discussing abstractions. "A party," he said, "is in one sense a joint stock association, in which those who contribute most direct the action and management of the concern. The slaveholders contributing in an overwhelming proportion to the capital strength of the Democratic party, they necessarily dictate and prescribe its policy. The inevitable caucus system enables them to do this with a show of fairness and justice." This class of slaveholders, consisting of only three hundred and forty-seven thousand persons, Seward went on to say, was spread from the banks of the Delaware to the banks of the Rio Grande; it possessed nearly all the real estate in that section, owned more than three million other "persons" who were denied all civil and political rights, and inhibited "freedom of speech, freedom of press, freedom of the ballot box, freedom of education, freedom of literature, and freedom of popular assemblies. . . . The slaveholding class has become the governing power in each of the slaveholding states and it practically chooses thirty of the sixty-two members of the Senate, ninety of the two hundred and thirty-three members of the House of Representatives, and one hundred and five of the two hundred and ninety-five electors of the President and Vice-President of the United States."

Becoming still more concrete, Seward accused the President of being "a confessed apologist of the slave-property class." Examining the composition of the Senate, he found the slave-owning group in possession of all the important committees. Peering into the House of Representatives he discovered no impregnable bulwark of freedom there. Nor did respect for judicial ermine compel him to spare the Supreme Court. With irony he exclaimed: "How fitting does the proclamation of its opening close with the invocation: 'God save the United States and this honorable court.' . . . The court consists of a chief justice and eight associate justices. Of these five were called from slave states and four from free states. The opinions and bias of each of them were carefully considered by the President and Senate when he was appointed. Not one of them was found wanting in soundness of politics, according to the slaveholder's exposition of the Constitution, and those who were called from the free states were even more distinguished in that respect than their brethren from the slaveholding states."

Seward then analyzed the civil service of the national government and could descry not a single person among the thousands employed in the post office, the treasury, and other great departments who was "false to the slaveholding interest." Under the spoils system, the dominion of the slavocracy extended into all branches of the federal administration. "The customs-houses and the public lands pour forth two golden streams—one into the elections to procure votes for the slaveholding class; and the other into the treasury to be enjoyed by those whom it shall see fit to reward with places in the public service." Even in the North, religion, learning, and the press were under the spell of this masterful class, frightened lest they incur its wrath.

Having described the gigantic operating structure of the slavocracy, Seward drew with equal power a picture of the opposing system founded on "free labor." He surveyed the course of economy in the North—the growth of industry, the spread of railways, the swelling tide of European immigration, and the westward roll of free farmers—rounding out the country, knitting it together, bringing "these antagonistic systems" continually into closer contact. Then he uttered those fateful words which startled conservative citizens from Maine to California—words of prophecy which proved to be brutally true—"the irrepressible conflict."

This inexorable clash, he said, was not "accidental, unnecessary, the work of interested or fanatical agitators and therefore ephemeral." No. "It is an irrepressible conflict between opposing and enduring forces." The hopes of those who sought peace by appealing to slave owners to reform themselves were as chaff in a storm. "How long and with what success have you waited already for that reformation? Did any property class ever so reform itself? Did the patricians in old Rome, the noblesse or clergy in France? The landholders in Ireland? The landed aristocracy in England? Does the slaveholding class even seek to beguile you with such a hope? Has it not become rapacious, arrogant, defiant?" All attempts at compromise were "vain and ephemeral." There was accordingly but one supreme task before the people of the United States—the task of confounding and overthrowing "by one decisive blow the betrayers of the Constitution and freedom forever." In uttering this indictment, this prophecy soon to be fulfilled with such appalling accuracy, Seward stepped beyond the bounds of cautious politics and read himself out of the little group of men who were eligible for the Republican nomination in 1860. Frantic efforts to soften his words by explanations and additions could not appease his critics.

Given an irrepressible conflict which could be symbolized in such unmistakable patterns by competent interpreters of opposing factions, a transfer of the issues from the forum to the field, from the conciliation of diplomacy to the decision of arms was bound to come. Each

54

side obdurately bent upon its designs and convinced of its rectitude, by the fulfillment of its wishes precipitated events and effected distributions of power that culminated finally in the tragedy foretold by Seward. Those Democrats who operated on historic knowledge rather than on prophetic insight, recalling how many times the party of Hamilton had been crushed at elections, remembering how the Whigs had never been able to carry the country on a cleancut Webster-Clay program, and counting upon the continued support of a huge array of farmers and mechanics marshaled behind the planters, imagined apparently that politics—viewed as the science of ballot enumeration—could resolve the problems of power raised by the maintenance of the Union.

And in this opinion they were confirmed by the outcome of the presidential campaign in 1852, when the Whigs, with General Winfield Scott, a hero of the Mexican war, at their head, were thoroughly routed by the Democratic candidate, General Franklin Pierce of New Hampshire. Indeed the verdict of the people was almost savage, for Pierce carried every state but four, receiving 254 out of 296 electoral votes. The Free-Soil party that branded slavery as a crime and called for its prohibition in the territories scarcely made a ripple, polling only 156,000 out of more than three million votes, a figure below the record set in the previous campaign.

With the Whigs beaten and the Free-Soilers evidently a dwindling handful of negligible critics, exultant Democrats took possession of the Executive offices and Congress, inspired by a firm belief that their tenure was secure. Having won an overwhelming victory on a definite tariff for revenue and pro-slavery program, they acted as if the party of Hamilton was for all practical purposes as powerless as the little band of abolitionist agitators. At the succeeding election in 1856 they again swept the country—this time with James Buchanan of Pennsylvania as their candidate. Though his triumph was not as magisterial as that of Pierce it was great enough to warrant a conviction that the supremacy of the Democratic party could not be broken at the polls.

During these eight years of tenure, a series of events occurred under Democratic auspices, which clinched the grasp of the planting interest upon the country and produced a correlative consolidation of the opposition. One line of development indicated an indefinite extension of the slave area; another the positive withdrawal of all government support from industrial and commercial enterprise. The first evidence of the new course came in the year immediately following the inauguration of Pierce. In 1854, Congress defiantly repealed the Missouri Compromise and threw open to slavery the vast section of the Louisiana Purchase which had been closed to it by the covenant adopted more than three decades before. On the instant came a rush of slavery champions from Missouri into Kansas determined to bring it into the southern sphere of influence. Not content with the conquest of the forbidden West, filibustering parties under pro-slavery leaders attempted to seize Cuba and Nicaragua and three American ministers abroad flung out to the world a flaming proclamation, known as the "Ostend Manifesto," which declared that the United States would be justified in wresting Cuba from Spain by force—acts of imperial aggression which even the Democratic administration in Washington felt constrained to repudiate.

Crowning the repeal of the Missouri Compromise came two decisions of the Supreme Court giving sanction to the expansion of slavery in America and assuring high protection for that peculiar institution even in the North. In the Dred Scott case decided in March, 1857, Chief Justice Taney declared in effect that the Missouri Compromise had been void from the beginning and that Congress had no power under the Constitution to prohibit slavery in the territories of the United States anywhere at any time. This legal triumph for the planting interest was followed in 1859 by another decision in which the Supreme Court upheld the fugitive slave law and all the drastic procedure provided for its enforcement. To the frightened abolitionists it seemed that only one more step was needed to make freedom unconstitutional throughout the country.

These extraordinary measures on behalf of slavery were accompanied by others that touched far more vitally economic interests in the North. In 1859, the last of the subsidies for trans-Atlantic steamship companies was ordered discontinued by Congress. In 1857, the tariff was again reduced, betraying an unmistakable drift of the nation toward free trade. In support of this action, the representatives of the South and Southwest were almost unanimous and they gathered into their fold a large number of New England congressmen on condition that no material reductions should be made in duties on cotton goods. On the other hand, the Middle States and the West offered a large majority against tariff reduction so that the division was symptomatic.

Immediately after the new revenue law went into effect an industrial panic burst upon the country, spreading distress among business men and free laborers. While that tempest was running high, the paper money anarchy let loose by the Democrats reached the acme of virulence as the notes of wildcat banks flooded the West and South and financial institutions crashed in every direction, fifty-one failing in Indiana alone within a period of five years. Since all hope of reviving

THE BREAKDOWN OF CONSENSUS

Hamilton's system of finance had been buried, those who believed that a sound currency was essential to national prosperity were driven to the verge of desperation. On top of these economic calamities came Buchanan's veto of the Homestead bill which the impatient agrarians had succeeded in getting through Congress in a compromise form—an act of presidential independence which angered the farmers and mechanics who regarded the national domain as their own inheritance. . . .

From what has just been said it must be apparent that the forces which produced the irrepressible conflict were very complex in nature and yet the momentous struggle has been so often reduced by historians to simple terms that a reexamination of the traditional thesis has become one of the tasks of the modern age. On the part of northern writers it was long the fashion to declare that slavery was the cause of the conflict between the states. Such for example was the position taken by James Ford Rhodes and made the starting point of his monumental work.

Assuming for the moment that this assertion is correct in a general sense, it will be easily observed even on a superficial investigation that "slavery" was no simple, isolated phenomenon. In itself it was intricate and it had filaments through the whole body economic. It was a labor system, the basis of planting, and the foundation of the southern aristocracy. That aristocracy, in turn, owing to the nature of its economic operations, resorted to public policies that were opposed to capitalism, sought to dominate the federal government, and, with the help of free farmers also engaged in agriculture, did at last dominate it. In the course of that political conquest, all the plans of commerce and industry for federal protection and subvention were overborne. It took more than a finite eye to discern where slavery as an ethical question left off and economics—the struggle over the distribution of wealth—began.

On the other hand, the early historians of the southern school, chagrined by defeat and compelled to face the adverse judgment of brutal fact, made the "rights of states"—something nobler than economics or the enslavement of Negroes—the issue for which the Confederacy fought and bled. That too like slavery seems simple until subjected to a little scrutiny. What is a state? At bottom it is a majority or perhaps a mere plurality of persons engaged in the quest of something supposed to be beneficial, or at all events not injurious, to the pursuers. And what are rights? Abstract, intangible moral values having neither substance nor form? The party debates over the economic issues of the middle period answer with an emphatic negative. If the southern planters had been content to grant tariffs, bounties, subsidies, and preferences to northern commerce and industry, it is not probable that they would have been molested in their most imperious proclamation of sovereignty.

But their theories and their acts involved interests more ponderable than political rhetoric. They threatened the country with secession first in defying the tariff of abominations and when they did secede thirty years later it was in response to the victory of a tariff and homestead party that proposed nothing more dangerous to slavery itself than the mere exclusion of the institution from the territories. It took more than a finite eye to discern where their opposition to the economic system of Hamilton left off and their affection for the rights of states began. The modern reader tossed about in a contrariety of opinions can only take his bearings by examining a few indubitable realities.

With reference to the popular northern view of the conflict, there stands the stubborn fact that at no time during the long gathering of the storm did Garrison's abolition creed rise to the dignity of a first rate political issue in the North. Nobody but agitators, beneath the contempt of the towering statesmen of the age, ever dared to advocate it. No great political organization even gave it the most casual indorsement.

When the abolitionists launched the Liberty party in the campaign of 1844 to work for emancipation, as we have noted, the voters answered their plea for "the restoration of equality of political rights among men" in a manner that demonstrated the invincible opposition of the American people. Out of more than two and a half million ballots cast in the election, only sixty-five thousands were recorded in favor of the Liberty candidate. That was America's answer to the call for abolition; and the advocates of that policy never again ventured to appeal to the electorate by presenting candidates on such a radical platform.

No other party organized between that time and the clash of arms attempted to do more than demand the exclusion of slavery from the territories and not until the Democrats by repealing the Missouri Compromise threatened to extend slavery throughout the West did any party poll more than a handful of votes on that issue. It is true that Van Buren on a free-soil platform received nearly three hundred thousand votes in 1848 but that was evidently due to personal influence, because his successor on a similar ticket four years afterward dropped into an insignificant place.

Even the Republican party, in the campaign of 1856, coming hard on the act of defiance which swept away the Missouri compact, won little more than one-third the active voters to the cause of restricting the slavery area. When transformed after four more years into a home-stead and high tariff party pledged merely to liberty in the territories, the Republicans polled a million votes fewer than the number cast for the opposing factions and rode into power on account of the divided ranks of the enemy. Such was the nation's reply to the anti-slavery agitation from the beginning of the disturbance until the cannon shot at Sumter opened a revolution.

Moreover not a single responsible statesman of the middle period committed himself to the doctrine of immediate and unconditional abolition to be achieved by independent political action. John Quincy Adams, ousted from the presidency by Jacksonian Democracy but returned to Washington as the Representative of a Massachusetts dis-trict in Congress, did declare that it was the duty of every free Ameri-can to work directly for the abolition of slavery and with uncanny vision foresaw that the knot might be cut with the sword. But Adams was regarded by astute party managers as a foolish and embittered old man and his prophecy as a dangerous delusion.

Practical politicians who felt the iron hand of the planters at Wash-ington—politicians who saw how deeply intertwined with the whole economic order the institution of slavery really was—could discover nothing tangible in immediate and unconditional abolition that ap-pealed to reason or came within the range of common sense. Lincoln was emphatic in assuring the slaveholders that no Republican had ever been detected in any attempt to disturb them. "We must not interfere with the institution of slavery in the states where it exists," he urged, "because the Constitution forbids it and the general welfare does not require us to do so."

Since, therefore, the abolition of slavery never appeared in the plat-form of any great political party, since the only appeal ever made to the electorate on that issue was scornfully repulsed, since the spokes-man of the Republicans emphatically declared that his party never intended to interfere with slavery in the states in any shape or form, it seems reasonable to assume that the institution of slavery was not the fundamental issue during the epoch preceding the bombardment of Fort Sumter. . . .

When the modern student examines all the verbal disputes over the nature of the Union—the arguments employed by the parties which operated and opposed the federal government between the adoption of the Constitution and the opening of the Civil War—he can hardly do otherwise than conclude that the linguistic devices used first on one side and then on the other were not derived from inherently neces-sary concepts concerning the intimate essence of the federal system.

The roots of the controversy lay elsewhere—in social groupings founded on differences in climate, soil, industries, and labor systems, in divergent social forces, rather than varying degrees of righteousness and wisdom, or what romantic historians call "the magnetism of great personalities."

12. AVERY CRAVEN: The Repressible Conflict*

Avery Craven's writings on the coming of the Civil War have had a great influence on modern historical scholarship. Professor Craven has been particularly interested in the psychological effects of political agitation; in his writings he has analyzed the way in which concrete issues became oversimplified into abstract symbols that inflamed the imaginations of men in the North and the South. The selection below is taken from The Repressible Conflict, 1830–61, *published by Avery Craven in 1939. As you read the selection consider the following questions:*

1. **According to Craven, what image of the South was being developed in the minds of the northern people?**
2. **What values and beliefs did the South develop in self-defence?**
3. **How much emphasis does Craven give to material values as compared to moral values in the developing crisis between the North and the South?**

Slavery as a reality and slavery as a symbol of southern life in its conflict with the North were . . . two quite different things. The one was important only as a very ancient labor system, probably at this time rather near the end of its existence; the other was a creation of inflamed imaginations which endowed southern men and institutions with every quality desired and extended its scope to cover all that was peculiar to the life of a section. The first was an economic fact, the other a psychological one. The first we can almost ignore in our study of sectional conflict; the second leaves few pages of history from 1830 to 1860 untouched.

For our present purposes we need only notice that in the period before 1820 slavery had been sharply criticized as a social feature by farseeing men in all sections of the nation. Northern states, finding it

* Reprinted with the permission of the publisher from pp. 76–91 of *The Repressible Conflict, 1830–1861,* by Avery Craven. Copyright 1939, Louisiana State University Press.

THE BREAKDOWN OF CONSENSUS

unprofitable and in conflict with their ideals as emphasized by the Revolution, had abolished it and southern leaders generally spoke of it as an institution which they confidently expected to pass in due season. The result was the localization of the institution, confining it to the South, and the creation of the idea that it was economically unprofitable and ethically unjustifiable. The colonization movement represented an effort to enable those who lived in areas where the number of Negroes, if freed, was great enough to present a race question to proceed with the work of manumission. It was to be a means of getting out of the frying pan without experiencing the unpleasantness of fire. Good men everywhere were expected to co-operate against a recognized evil. Only now and then did some stray voice dissent.

The debates over the Missouri Compromise brought the first indications that earlier attitudes were changing. They produced sharp condemnation of slavery and even the suggestion that Congress had the power to destroy it. Radicals, like Livermore of New Hampshire, asked: "How will the desire for wealth render us blind to the sin of holding both the bodies and souls of our fellow men in chains. . . . Do not, for the sake of cotton and tobacco, let it be told to future ages that, while pretending to love liberty, we have purchased an extensive country to disgrace it with the foulest reproach of nations!" Senator King of New York went so far as to insist that "no human law, compact, or compromise can establish or continue slavery. . . . There is no such thing as a slave."

Southern men, in turn, defended themselves, and a few began the partial defense of their institution. Most of them could have said with Reed of Georgia: "Believe me, sir, I am not a panegyrist of slavery. It is an unnatural state; a dark cloud which obscures half the lustre of our free institutions." All of them did agree with Barbour of Virginia who insisted that his opponent overstated its ills! "He has shaded it too deeply, with the coloring of his own imagination," he said. But a few, like William Smith of South Carolina, "justified slavery on the broadest principles, without qualification or reserve." He pronounced it "right" and viewed it "as a benefit" which would be perpetuated.

The attack on slavery as a sectional institution had been launched; the proslavery argument as a sectional defense had been begun.

It is not necessary to follow the development of these two positions in the purely domestic conflicts in the several southern states. Nor need we do more than point out the widening national statement evolved in the contests over antislavery petitions in Congress and the sending of inflammatory materials through the mails. The effects were only to sharpen the opposing positions and to increase the sectional character of both attack and defense.

The rise of the professional spokesmen—called "abolitionists" on the one side and "fire-eaters" on the other—needs notice only because of the emotional flavor which they added to the contest. William Lloyd Garrison had the gift for making everyone mad—including himself. He had an unusual capacity for hating. If Southerners like Dew and Harper and Ruffin were more dignified and logical, they were no less positive and one-sided. When the clergymen entered the field, and thousands of them did, they added righteous indignation to the conflict. The clan is notoriously efficient in uncompromising assertion of "right" and "wrong." When one speaks for God, argument is useless; only combat is possible.

The significant thing about the antislavery men and movements and those who developed the abstract defense of the South is the picture of slavery and of society which they created. They were too extreme for any great following. Conservative men of the day dismissed them as fanatics and hastened to assure their friends in other sections that such voices did not represent the true opinions and feelings of their people. But these fanatics, unrestrained by fact, were creating clear-cut pictures of slavery, slaves, slaveholders, and southern and northern life positive enough to suit the needs of those engaged in conflict. When politicians became enraged in debate, when the sections became entangled in strife, then these pictures were to serve wider purposes. The time would come when opponents needed just such distorted weapons—when false propaganda could take the place of truth. Then the conceptions of men and societies woven by these intense emotional voices of heaven would pass as sober truth. Enemies would become devils; friends, the incarnation of right and justice. Blood would have to be spilled.

The antislavery impulse as directed against that institution in the South began in the 1820's and lasted until emancipation and victory in battle brought it to an end. It passed through several distinct stages, the earlier ones being more or less pure social reform in character and the later ones so badly mixed with politics that it is difficult to tell what is political, what social, and what moral. It worked through every medium of individual and group contact known to the day and appealed to interest, conscience, emotion, and reason. Little children learned their A B C's from booklets which read:

> A is an Abolitionist,
> A man who wants to free
> The wretched slave—and give to all
> An equal liberty.

B is a Brother with a skin
Of somewhat darker hue,
But in our Heavenly Father's sight
He is as dear as you.

C is the Cotton field, to which
This injured brother's driven,
When, as the white man's *slave*, he toils
From early morn 'till even.

D is the Driver, cold and stern,
Who follows, whip in hand,
To punish those who dare to rest
Or disobey command.

And so on down through:

K is the Kidnapper, who stole
That little child and mother—
Shrieking, it clung around her, but
He tore them from each other.

L is the Lash, that brutally
He swung around its head,
Threatening that "if it cried again,
He'd whip it 'till 'twas dead."

And at the bitter end:

Z is a zealous man, sincere,
Truthful, and just and true;
An earnest pleader for the slave—
Will you not be so too?

With this as a beginning the work of indoctrination was carried on by local and national organizations through means which ranged from songs and stories, pamphlets and books, conventions and lobbies, to the violent speeches of a Charles Sumner in the Senate or the more subtle statements of a Lincoln on the hustings in Illinois pointing out the moral wrong in human bondage and insisting that it be put on the road to ultimate extinction.

But regardless of time and place, type of antislavery men or form of appeal, two great facts were being impressed upon the northern people: first, the Southerner was an aristocrat, an enemy of democracy in society and government; and second, he was a man of violent and generally uncontrolled passions which led him into intemperance, licentiousness, brutality, and disregard of others' rights. Most Southerners were supposed to be slaveholders and, as such, they constituted a single interest, which could be designated as *The Slave Power,* whose purpose was the rule or the ruin of the whole Union. As the *Philanthropist* said in 1840: "All the great changes of policy which have successfully involved in disaster each and every northern interest have been introduced by the dictation of the Slave Power."

In the widely read pamphlet entitled *American Slavery As It Is,* a writer spoke of the "savage ferocity" of southern men as "the natural result of their habit of daily plundering and oppressing the slave." He tells of perpetual idleness broken only by brutal cockfights, gander pullings, and horse races so barbarous in character that "the blood of the tortured animal drips from the lash and flies at every leap from the stroke of the rowel." *Anti-Slavery Tract Number 7* declared that "a million and a half of slave women, some of them without even the tinge of African blood, are given up, a lawful prey to the unbridled lusts of their masters." Theodore Parker supplied the comment on this text by saying: "The South is full of mulattoes; its best 'blood flows in the veins of slaves.' . . . Girls, the children of mulattoes, are sold at great prices, as food for private licentiousness, or public furniture in houses of ill-fame." The *Liberator* referred to Southerners as "sagacious desperadoes and remorseless men-stealers"; and the section as "ferocious and despotic." Garrison insisted that it was as easy to "transform wolves and hyenas into lambs and doves" as to appeal to southern "understandings, consciences and hearts." He topped it all by saying: "We would sooner trust the honor of the country . . . in the hands of inmates of our penitentiaries and prisons than in their hands. . . . They are the meanest thieves and the worst of robbers. . . . We do not acknowledge them to be within the pale of Christianity, of republicanism, of humanity."

In such a picture, slavery was one round of cruelty. David L. Child honestly stated: "From all that I have read and heard upon the subject of whipping done by masters and overseers to slaves . . . I have come to the conclusion that some hundreds of *cart whip* and cowskin instruments, which I am told make the skin fly feathers, and cut frequently to the bone, are in *perpetual daily motion* in the slave states." Charles Sumner's impressions, if we can judge by his speeches in Congress, were almost as harsh. Nor did he manifest the slightest interest in gaining better ones when the good Francis Lieber, himself an antislavery man, informed him that "my wife read [your speech] . . . and exclaimed at the picture you give of slavery, 'How untrue.' It seems to me slavery may be attacked without fiction such as you state. . . ."

The final logical conclusion of all this discussion was stated by Theodore Parker in 1851 when he declared that:

> The South, in the main, had a very different origin from the North. I think few if any persons settled there for religion's sake; or for the sake of the freedom of the State. It was not a moral idea which sent men to Virginia, Georgia, or Carolina. "Men do not gather grapes of thorns." The difference in the seed will appear in the difference of the crop. In the character of the people of the North, and South, it appears at this day. . . . Here, now, is the great cause of the difference in the material results, represented in towns and villages, by farms and factories, ships and shops. Here is the cause of differences in the schools and colleges, churches, and in the literature; the cause of difference in men. The South with its despotic idea, dishonors labor, but wishes to compromise between its idleness and its appetite, and so kidnaps men to do its work.

"Two opposing civilizations are in conflict here, and have been from the infancy of our Union," said Professor Austin Phelps of Andover Theological Seminary.

The full effect of such distortion was not apparent at once. The historian can judge its real force only on that bitter July day in 1861 when the *New York Herald* carried to a receptive nation the story of southern atrocities committed on the battlefield at Bull Run.

> A private of the First Connecticut Regiment found a wounded rebel lying in the sun, and lifted him up and carried him to a shade, where he gently layed him and gave him to drink from his canteen. Revived by the drink, the ingrate drew his pistol and shot his benefactor through the heart. Another instance is related of a troop of rebel cavalry deliberately firing upon a number of wounded men, who had been placed together in the shade. . . . It is said by Virginians who have come from the battlefield that these fiends in human shape have taken the bayonets and knives of our wounded and dying soldiers and thrust them into their hearts and left them sticking there, and that some of the Louisiana Zouaves have severed the heads of our dead from their bodies, and amused themselves by kicking them about as footballs.

All of which, as the *Cincinnati Enquirer* added, was "attributable to the barbarism of slavery, in which and to which the southern soldiers have been educated. . . ."

For a generation southern men and women lived under such an attack. It began, as we have said, as a simple questioning of the justice of human slavery by a few earnest, if fanatical, humanitarians. It ended on the level of a high moral crusade, the justice of which few northern men questioned, and tended to include in its sweep of purpose the overthrow of the whole southern way of life. Garrison and Phillips and Parker became as well known in the South as in the North. In fact, one writer has recently evaluated Garrison in the antislavery impulse as more important for the hatred he stirred below Mason and Dixon's line than for the influence he wielded above it. Gradually the South became conscious and bitter. It turned in self-defense. A "refutation of the calumnies circulated against" the section appeared almost as soon as the attack was begun. It showed that emotions had been stirred and revealed the possibility of a sectional response. Edwin Holland asked his neighbors to present facts in refutation of charges made, and referred to the "abundant testimony of the hostile and unfriendly spirit with which the most vital interests" of the South were discussed. He declared that "the North and East" were "or affected to be, totally ignorant of the actual state and character of our Negro population; they represent the condition of their bondage as a perpetual revolution of labor and severity, rendered still more deplorable by an utter destitution of all the comforts of life. . . ." He charged "malignity of design" and "utter contempt of truth in such statements" and declared them uttered without "the most ordinary regard of our feelings."

By 1854 the Macon *Georgia Telegraph* could say that "the grand question . . . is what shall be done to protect the South from this everlasting enmity and turmoil, which tears the country to pieces . . . when any question arises which . . . affects the question of slavery." It felt the Union could stand anything but

> the insolent and insidious rust of a progressing, perverted, and corrupt public opinion, which we know has been manufactured with more than Jesuitical zeal and perseverance for a quarter of a century in a portion of this Confederacy. The pseudo ministry . . . of our country . . . to take the child's young mind and preoccupy it by many species of lying and blasphemous outcry . . . and follow the child into manhood with this sort of teaching as regards Southern people, until lies and sophistry and false information about us have become ingrained into the very intellect and hearts of Northern people.

A more positive reply was offered in the ingenious "proslavery argument" which was evolved in the South from 1820 to 1860. From a half-apologetic defense of slavery as a necessary evil, it grew to an aggressive glorification of a way of life. The Bible, the Past, Nature, and Civilization were all appealed to, and when the task was completed the Southerner stood before the world a superior man in a superior society. An early group attempted to point out the benefits of slavery to the Negro himself. The Reverend J. C. Stiles showed that slavery had turned twice as many heathens into Christians as all other missionary efforts combined, and Reverend Stringfellow was certain that God had confined the institution to the South because of the superior qualities in its people for lifting ignorant Negroes to culture! Others pointed out the inability of the Negro to be of economic benefit to himself and society without the supervision and direction which slavery afforded. A few with a scientific bent, such as Van Everie and Nott, insisted on the unique origins of the Negro and his peculiar physical and mental traits which predestined him to servitude. The clergy, even then a bit skeptical of science, accepted the differences pointed out, but explained them by the curse of God on Ham.

From such beginnings, the defense went on to ingenious refinements, as men discovered that slaves were better off than factory workers; that all labor, regardless of the system, was exploited; that republican government could exist only where all white men were free from drudgery; and that without slavery in agriculture all farmers were destined to a degrading peasantry. It reached its fullness in the staunch belief that under slavery, the South had achieved a vastly superior civilization, toward which the rest of the world must move. Here was a society without a labor conflict, without race conflict, and without social agitation. There was no unemployment and no old-age worries for its toilers. Culture and refinement prevailed, and the ruin which urban life produced in "depravity of morals . . . increase of want, and of crime," as Edward Fisher charged, was lacking. Slavery had marked the beginning of man's upward climb, as Professor Dew had early declared, and it now marked its highest peak. When war broke, the Reverend J. H. Thornwell could say:

> The parties in this conflict are not merely abolitionists and slaveholders; they are atheists, socialists, communists, red republicans, jacobins on the one side, and the friends of order and regulated freedom on the other. In one word, the world is the battle ground, Christianity and atheism the combatants, and the progress of humanity the stake.

What stands out in all this is the belief in the peculiar quality and character of the South; the growing emotion involved in attack and defense; the assumption of differences inherent and persistent. There was a North, and there was a South. They represented entirely different values and qualities. They were by nature enemies. And, what is most significant, *moral* values were involved—things affecting humanity, civilization, God's purposes in this world. Those are things for which men give their lives; for which holy wars are fought. National consciousness is woven from fear and resentment as well as from conviction and faith. Material realities shrink into insignificance when brought into comparison.

13. ALLAN NEVINS: "Great and Complex Events Have Great and Complex Causes"*

Allan Nevins is the author of the latest large-scale history of the Civil War era. His volumes entitled The Ordeal of the Union *(two vols., 1947) and* The Emergence of Lincoln *(two vols., 1950) are the most comprehensive treatment of the pre-Civil War period by a modern scholar. The following selection is the concluding section of* The Emergence of Lincoln *in which Nevins summarizes his views on the causes of the civil conflict in America. Read the selection carefully and consider the following questions:*

1. **What explanation for the drift to war does Nevins think is the flimsiest?**
2. **How does Nevins assess the role of politicians and publicists who fomented sectional hysteria?**
3. **What, in Nevins' explanation, is the fundamental factor that caused the breakdown in the American consensus?**

Great and complex events have great and complex causes. Burke, in his *Reflections on the Revolution in France,* wrote that "a state without the means of some change is without the means of its conservation," and that a constant reconciliation of "the two principles of conservation and correction" is indispensable to healthy national growth. It is safe to say that every such revolutionary era as that on which the

* Reprinted with the permission of Charles Scribner's Sons from *The Emergence of Lincoln,* Vol. II, pp. 462–471, by Allan Nevins. Copyright 1950 by Charles Scribner's Sons.

United States entered in 1860 finds its genesis in an inadequate adjustment of these two forces. It is also safe to say that when a tragic national failure occurs, it is largely a failure of leadership. "Brains are of three orders," wrote Machiavelli, "those that understand of themselves, those that understand when another shows them, and those that understand neither by themselves nor by the showing of others." Ferment and change must steadily be controlled; the real must, as Bryce said, be kept resting on the ideal; and if disaster is to be avoided, wise leaders must help thoughtless men to understand, and direct the action of invincibly ignorant men. Necessary reforms may be obstructed in various ways; by sheer inertia, by tyranny and class selfishness, or by the application of compromise to basic principles—this last being in Lowell's view the main cause of the Civil War. Ordinarily the obstruction arises from a combination of all these elements. To explain the failure of American leadership in 1846–1861, and the revolution that ensued, is a bafflingly complicated problem.

Looking backward from the verge of war in March, 1861, Americans could survey a series of ill-fated decisions by their chosen agents. One unfortunate decision was embodied in Douglas's Kansas-Nebraska Act of 1854. Had an overwhelming majority of Americans been ready to accept the squatter sovereignty principle, this law might have proved a statesmanlike stroke; but it was so certain that powerful elements North and South would resist it to the last that it accentuated the strife and confusion. Another disastrous decision was made by Taney and his associates in the Dred Scott pronouncement of 1857. Still another was made by Buchanan when he weakly accepted the Lecompton Constitution and tried to force that fraudulent document through Congress. The Northern legislatures which passed Personal Liberty Acts made an unhappy decision. Most irresponsible, wanton, and disastrous of all was the decision of those Southern leaders who in 1858–60 turned to the provocative demand for Congressional protection of slavery in all the Territories of the republic. Still other errors might be named. Obviously, however, it is the forces behind these decisions which demand our study; the waters pouring down the gorge, not the rocks which threw their spray into the air.

At this point we meet a confused clamor of voices as various students attempt an explanation of the tragic denouement of 1861. Some writers are as content with a simple explanation as Lord Clarendon was when he attributed the English Civil War to the desire of Parliament for an egregious domination of the government. The bloody conflict, declared James Ford Rhodes, had "a single cause, slavery." He was but echoing what Henry Wilson and other early historians had written, that the aggressions of the Slave Power offered the central explanation. That opinion had been challenged as early as 1861 by the London *Saturday Review*, which remarked that "slavery is but a surface question in American politics," and by such Southern propagandists as Yancey, who tried to popularize a commercial theory of the war, emphasizing a supposed Southern revolt against the tariff and other Yankee exactions. A later school of writers was to find the key to the tragedy in an inexorable conflict between the business-minded North and the agrarian-minded South, a thrusting industrialism colliding with a rather static agricultural society. Still another group of writers has accepted the theory that the war resulted from psychological causes. They declare that agitators, propagandists, and alarmists on both sides, exaggerating the real differences of interest, created a state of mind, a hysterical excitement, which made armed conflict inevitable.

At the very outset of the war Senator Mason of Virginia, writing to his daughter, asserted that two systems of society were in conflict; systems, he implied, as different as those of Carthage and Rome, Protestant Holland and Catholic Spain. That view, too, was later to be elaborated by a considerable school of writers. Two separate nations, they declared, had arisen within the United States in 1861, much as two separate nations had emerged within the first British Empire by 1776. Contrasting ways of life, rival group consciousness, divergent hopes and fears made a movement for separation logical; and the minority people, believing its peculiar civilization in danger of suppression, began a war for independence. We are told, indeed, that two types of nationalism came into conflict: a Northern nationalism which wished to preserve the unity of the whole republic, and a Southern nationalism intent on creating an entirely new republic.

It is evident that some of these explanations deal with merely superficial phenomena, and that others, when taken separately, represent but subsidiary elements in the play of forces. Slavery was a great fact; the demands of Northern industrialism constituted a great fact; sectional hysteria was a great fact. But do they not perhaps relate themselves to some profounder underlying cause? This question has inspired one student to suggest that "the confusion of a growing state" may offer the fundamental explanation of the drift to war; an unsatisfactory hypothesis, for westward growth, railroad growth, business growth, and cultural growth, however much attended with "confusion," were unifying factors, and it was not the new-made West but old-settled South Carolina which led in the schism.

One fact needs emphatic statement: of all the monistic explanations for the drift to war, that posited upon supposed economic causes is the flimsiest. This theory was sharply rejected at the time by so astute an observer as Alexander H. Stephens. South Carolina, he wrote his brother on New Year's Day, 1861, was seceding from a tariff "which is just what her own Senators and members in Congress made it." As for the charges of consolidation and despotism made by some Carolinians, he thought they arose from peevishness rather than a calm analysis of facts. "The truth is, the South, almost in mass, has voted, I think, for every measure of general legislation that has passed both houses and become law for the last ten years." The South, far from groaning under tyranny, had controlled the government almost from its beginning, and Stephens believed that its only real grievance lay in the Northern refusal to return fugitive slaves and to stop the anti-slavery agitation. "All other complaints are founded on threatened dangers which may never come, and which I feel very sure would be averted if the South would pursue a judicious and wise course." Stephens was right. It was true that the whole tendency of Federal legislation 1842–1860 was toward free trade; true that the tariff in force when secession began was largely Southern-made; true that it was the lowest tariff the country had known since 1816; true that it cost a nation of thirty million people but sixty million dollars in indirect revenue; true that without secession no new tariff law, obnoxious to the Democratic Party, could have passed before 1863—if then.

In the official explanations which one Southern State after another published for its secession, economic grievances are either omitted entirely or given minor position. There were few such supposed grievances which the agricultural States of Illinois, Iowa, Indiana, Wisconsin, and Minnesota did not share with the South—and they never threatened to secede. Charles A. Beard finds the tap-root of the war in the resistance of the planter interest to Northern demands enlarging the old Hamilton-Webster policy. The South was adamant in standing for "no high protective tariffs, no ship subsidies, no national banking and currency system; in short, none of the measures which business enterprise deemed essential to its progress." But the Republican platform in 1856 was silent on the tariff; in 1860 it carried a milk-and-water statement on the subject which Western Republicans took, mild as it was, with a wry face; the incoming President was little interested in the tariff; and any harsh legislation was impossible. Ship subsidies were not an issue in the campaign of 1860. Neither were a national banking system and a national currency system. They were not mentioned in the Republican platform nor discussed by party debaters. The Pacific Railroad was advocated both by the Douglas Democrats and the Republicans; and it is noteworthy that Seward and Douglas were for building both a Northern and a Southern line. In short, the divisive economic issues are easily exaggerated. At the same time, the unifying economic factors were both numerous and powerful. North and South had economies which were largely complementary. It was no misfortune to the South that Massachusetts cotton mills wanted its staple, and that New York ironmasters like Hewitt were eager to sell rails dirt-cheap to Southern railway builders; and sober businessmen on both sides, merchants, bankers, and manufacturers, were the men most anxious to keep the peace and hold the Union together.

We must seek further for an explanation; and in so doing, we must give special weight to the observations of penetrating leaders of the time, who knew at firsthand the spirit of the people. Henry J. Raymond, moderate editor of the New York *Times*, a sagacious man who disliked Northern abolitionists and Southern radicals, wrote in January, 1860, an analysis of the impending conflict which attributed it to a competition for power:

> In every country there must be a just and equal balance of powers in the government, an equal distribution of the national forces. Each section and each interest must exercise its due share of influence and control. It is always more or less difficult to preserve their just equipoise, and the larger the country, and the more varied its great interests, the more difficult does the task become, and the greater the shock and disturbance caused by an attempt to adjust it when once disturbed. I believe I state only what is generally conceded to be a fact, when I say that the growth of the Northern States in population, in wealth, in all the elements of political influence and control, has been out of proportion to their political influence in the Federal Councils. While the Southern States have less than a third of the aggregate population of the Union, their interests have influenced the policy of the government far more than the interests of the Northern States. . . . Now the North has made rapid advances within the last five years, and it naturally claims a proportionate share of influence and power in the affairs of the Confederacy.
>
> It is inevitable that this claim should be put forward, and it is also inevitable that it should be conceded. No party can long resist it; it overrides all parties, and makes them the mere instruments of its will. It is quite as strong today in the heart of the Democratic party of the North as in the Republican ranks; and any party which ignores it will lose its hold on the public mind.
>
> Why does the South resist this claim? Not because it is unjust in itself, but because it has become involved with the

question of slavery, and has drawn so much of its vigor and vitality from that quarter, that it is almost merged in that issue. The North bases its demand for increased power, in a very great degree, on the action of the government in regard to slavery—and the just and rightful ascendency of the North in the Federal councils comes thus to be regarded as an element of danger to the institutions of the Southern States.

In brief, Raymond, who held that slavery was a moral wrong, that its economic and social tendencies were vicious, and that the time had come to halt its growth with a view to its final eradication, believed that the contest was primarily one for power, and for the application of that power to the slave system. With this opinion Alexander H. Stephens agreed: the Georgian said he believed slavery both morally and politically right. In his letter to Lincoln on December 30, 1860, he declared that the South did not fear that the new Republican Administration would interfere directly and immediately with slavery in the States. What Southerners did fear was the ultimate result of the shift of power which had just occurred—in its application to slavery:

Now this subject, which is confessedly on all sides outside of the constitutional action of the Government, so far as the States are concerned, is made the "central idea" in the platform of principles announced by the triumphant party. The leading object seems to be simply, and wantonly, if you please, to put the institutions of nearly half the States under the ban of public opinion and national condemnation. This, upon general principles, is quite enough of itself to arouse a spirit not only of general indignation, but of revolt on the part of the proscribed. Let me illustrate. It is generally conceded by the Republicans even, that Congress cannot interfere with slavery in the States. It is equally conceded that Congress cannot establish any form of religious worship. Now suppose that any one of the present Christian churches or sects prevailed in all the Southern States, but had no existence in any one of the Northern States,—under such circumstances suppose the people of the Northern States should organize a political party, not upon a foreign or domestic policy, but with one leading idea of condemnation of the doctrines and tenets of that particular church, and with an avowed object of preventing its extension into the common Territories, even after the highest judicial tribunal of the land had decided they had no such constitutional power. And suppose that a party so organized should carry a Presidential election. Is it not apparent that a general feeling of resistance to the success, aims, and objects of such a party would necessarily and rightfully ensue?

Raymond and Stephens agreed that the two sections were competing for power; that a momentous transfer of power had just occurred; and that it held fateful consequences because it was involved with the issue of slavery, taking authority from a section which believed slavery moral and healthy, and giving it to a section which held slavery immoral and pernicious. To Stephens this transfer was ground for resuming the ultimate sovereignty of the States. Here we find a somewhat more complex statement of James Ford Rhodes's thesis that the central cause of the Civil War lay in slavery. Here, too, we revert to the assertions of Yancey and Lincoln that the vital conflict was between those who thought slavery right and those who thought it wrong. But this definition we can accept only if we probe a little deeper for a concept which both modifies and enlarges the basic source of perplexity and quarrel.

The main root of the conflict (and there were minor roots) was the problem of slavery *with its complementary problem of race-adjustment;* the main source of the tragedy was the refusal of either section to face these conjoined problems squarely and pay the heavy costs of a peaceful settlement. Had it not been for the difference in race, the slavery issue would have presented no great difficulties. But as the racial gulf existed, the South inarticulately but clearly perceived that elimination of this issue would still leave it the terrible problem of the Negro. Those historians who write that if slavery had simply been left alone it would soon have withered overlook this heavy impediment. The South as a whole in 1846–61 was not moving toward emancipation, but away from it. It was not relaxing the laws which guarded the system, but reinforcing them. It was not ameliorating slavery, but making it harsher and more implacable. The South was further from a just solution of the slavery problem in 1830 than it had been in 1789. It was further from a tenable solution in 1860 than it had been in 1830. Why was it going from bad to worse? Because Southern leaders refused to nerve their people to pay the heavy price of race-adjustment. These leaders never made up their mind to deal with the problem as the progressive temper of civilization demanded. They would not adopt the new outlook which the upward march of mankind required because they saw that the gradual abolition of slavery would bring a measure of political privilege; that political privilege would usher in a measure of economic equality; that on the heels of economic equality would come a rising social status for the Negro. Southern leadership dared not ask the people to pay this price.

A heavy responsibility for the failure of America in this period rests with this Southern leadership, which lacked imagination, ability, and

THE BREAKDOWN OF CONSENSUS

courage. But the North was by no means without its full share, for the North equally refused to give a constructive examination to the central question of slavery as linked with race adjustment. This was because of two principal reasons. Most abolitionists and many other sentimental-minded Northerners simply denied that the problem existed. Regarding all Negroes as white men with dark skins, whom a few years of schooling would bring abreast of the dominant race, they thought that no difficult adjustment was required. A much more numerous body of Northerners would have granted that a great and terrible task of race adjustment existed—but they were reluctant to help shoulder any part of it. Take a million or two million Negroes into the Northern States? Indiana, Illinois, and even Kansas were unwilling to take a single additional person of color. Pay tens of millions to help educate and elevate the colored population? Take even a first step by offering to pay the Southern slaveholders some recompense for a gradual liberation of their human property? No Northern politician dared ask his constituents to make so unpopular a sacrifice. The North, like the South, found it easier to drift blindly toward disaster.

The hope of solving the slavery problem without a civil war rested upon several interrelated factors, of which one merits special emphasis. We have said that the South as a whole was laboring to bolster and stiffen slavery—which was much to its discredit. But it is nevertheless true that slavery was dying all around the edges of its domain; it was steadily decaying in Delaware, Maryland, western Virginia, parts of Kentucky, and Missouri. Much of the harshness of Southern legislation in the period sprang from a sense that slavery was in danger from *internal* weaknesses. In no great time Delaware, Maryland, and Missouri were likely to enter the column of free States; and if they did, reducing the roster to twelve, the doom of the institution would be clearly written. Allied with this factor was the rapid comparative increase of Northern strength, and the steady knitting of economic, social, and moral ties between the North and West, leaving the South in a position of manifest inferiority. A Southern Confederacy had a fair fighting chance in 1861; by 1880 it would have had very little. If secession could have been postponed by two decades, natural forces might well have placed a solution full in sight. Then, too, the growing pressure of world sentiment must in time have produced its effect. But to point out these considerations is not to suggest that in 1861 a policy of procrastination and appeasement would have done anything but harm. All hope of bringing Southern majority sentiment to a better attitude would have been lost if Lincoln and his party had flinched on the basic issue of the restriction of slavery; for by the seventh decade of nineteenth century history, the time had come when that demand had to be maintained.

While in indicting leadership we obviously indict the public behind the leaders, we must also lay some blame upon a political environment which gave leadership a poor chance. American parties, under the pressure of sectional feeling, worked badly. The government suffered greatly, moreover, from the lack of any adequate planning agency. Congress was not a truly deliberative body, and its committees had not yet learned to do long-range planning. The President might have formulated plans, but he never did. For one reason, no President between Polk and Lincoln had either the ability or the prestige required; for another reason, Fillmore, Pierce, and Buchanan all held that their duty was merely to execute the laws, not to initiate legislation. Had the country possessed a ministerial form of government, the Cabinet in leading the legislature would have been compelled to lay down a program of real scope concerning slavery. As it was, leadership in Washington was supplied only spasmodically by men like Clay, Douglas, and Crittenden.

And as we have noted, the rigidity of the American system was at this time a grave handicap. Twice, in the fall of 1854 and of 1858, the elections gave a stunning rebuke to the Administration. Under a ministerial system, the old government would probably have gone out and a new one have come in. In 1854, however, Pierce continued to carry on the old policies, and in 1858 Buchanan remained the drearily inept helmsman of the republic. Never in our history were bold, quick planning and a flexible administration of policy more needed; never was the failure to supply them more complete.

Still another element in the tragic chronicle of the time must be mentioned. Much that happens in human affairs is accidental. When a country is guided by true statesmen the role of accident is minimized; when it is not, unforeseen occurrences are numerous and dangerous. In the summer and fall of 1858, as we have seen, the revival of a conservative opposition party in the upper South, devoted to the Union, furnished a real gleam of hope. If this opposition had been given unity and determined leadership, if moderate Southerners had stood firm against the plot of Yancey and others to disrupt the Democratic Party, if Floyd had been vigilant enough to read the warning letter about John Brown and act on it, the situation might even then have been saved. Instead, John Brown's mad raid fell on public opinion like a thunderstroke, exasperating men everywhere and dividing North and South more tragically than ever. The last chance of persuading the South to submit to an essential step, the containment of slavery, was gone.

The war, when it came, was not primarily a conflict over State Rights, although that issue had become involved in it. It was not primarily a war born of economic grievances, although many Southerners had been led to think that they were suffering, or would soon suffer, economic wrongs. It was not a war created by politicians and publicists who fomented hysteric excitement; for while hysteria was important, we have always to ask what basic reasons made possible the propaganda which aroused it. It was not primarily a war about slavery alone, although that institution seemed to many the grand cause. It was a war over slavery *and* the future position of the Negro race in North America. Was the Negro to be allowed, as a result of the shift of power signalized by Lincoln's election, to take the first step toward an ultimate position of general economic, political, and social equality with the white man? Or was he to be held immobile in a degraded, servile position, unchanging for the next hundred years as it had remained essentially unchanged for the hundred years past? These questions were implicit in Lincoln's demand that slavery be placed in a position where the public mind could rest assured of its ultimate extinction.

Evasion by the South, evasion by the North, were no longer possible. The alternatives faced were an unpopular but curative adjustment of the situation by the opposed parties, or a war that would force an adjustment upon the loser. For Americans in 1861, as for many other peoples throughout history, war was easier than wisdom and courage.

Now that you have completed the readings in this volume, a good way for you to organize what you have learned is to write a paper on these questions:

Part 6

Was the American consensus destroyed because of an irreconcilable moral division over the issue of slavery between the North and the South — or was the debate over slavery a disguise for other purposes? If so, what were such other purposes? Did they include a thirst for power by fanatical politicians, or the northern industrialists' drive for profit and power?

Conclusion

If you wish to do more reading and research before you write such a paper, the following books would be helpful.

I. Source Materials, Speeches, and Memoirs

Paul M. Angle (ed.), *Created Equal? The Complete Lincoln-Douglas Debates of 1858.* 1958.

—— *The Lincoln Reader.* 1947.

Henry S. Commager, *Documents of American History.* 1958. (Especially Doc. Nos. 174–199.)

Kirk H. Porter and Donald B. Johnson (comps.), *National Party Platforms 1840–1956.* 1956.

James D. Richardson (ed.), *Compilation of the Messages and Papers of the President, 1789–1897.* Vol. 5. 1907.

II. Historical Interpretations, Biographies, and Special Studies

Gerald N. Capers, *John C. Calhoun, Opportunist.* 1960.

—— *Stephen A. Douglas, Defender of the Union.* 1959.

Margaret L. Coit, *John C. Calhoun, American Portrait.* 1950.

Arthur C. Cole, *The Irrepressible Conflict, 1850–1865.* 1934.

Andrew W. Crandall, *Early History of the Republican Party, 1854–1856.* 1930.

Avery O. Craven, *Civil War in the Making, 1815–1860*. 1959.

—— *The Growth of Southern Nationalism, 1848–1861*. 1953.

Richard N. Current, *Daniel Webster and the Rise of National Conservatism*. 1955.

Philip S. Foner, *Business and Slavery: The New York Merchants and the Irrepressible Conflict*. 1941.

Norman A. Graebner (ed.), *Politics and the Crisis of 1860*. 1961.

George F. Milton, *The Eve of Conflict: Stephen A. Douglas and the Needless War*. 1934.

Allan Nevins, *Ordeal of the Union*. 2 vols. 1947.

—— *The Emergence of Lincoln*. 2 vols. 1950.

Roy F. Nichols, *The Disruption of American Democracy*. 1948.

Rollin G. Osterweis, *Romanticism and Nationalism in the Old South*. 1949.

Ulrich B. Phillips, *The Course of the South to Secession: An Interpretation*. 1939.

James G. Randall, *Civil War and Reconstruction*. 1953.

Edwin C. Rozwenc (ed.), *The Causes of the American Civil War*. 1961.

Henry H. Simms, *A Decade of Sectional Controversy*. 1942.

Kenneth M. Stampp, *And the War Came: The North and the Secession Crisis, 1860–1861*. 1950.

—— *The Causes of the Civil War*. 1959.

Benjamin P. Thomas, *Abraham Lincoln*. 1952.